univ

THE UNIVERSITY OF EDINBURGH
An illustrated history

ydz69@cam.ac.uk

ydz69@cam.ac.uk

Yanjun Diao X

"Yengin" +80 13609297560

D0891187

THE UNIVERSITY OF EDINBURGH
An illustrated history

Robert D. Anderson, Michael Lynch and Nicholas Phillipson

EDINBURGH
UNIVERSITY
PRESS

© The University of Edinburgh, 2003

Edinburgh University Press Ltd
22 George Square, Edinburgh

Typeset in Bembo
Design by Mark Blackadder
Printed and bound in Great Britain by
The University Press, Cambridge

A CIP record for this book is
available from the British Library

ISBN 0 7486 1645 4 (hardback)
ISBN 0 7486 1646 2 (paperback)

The right of Robert D. Anderson,
Michael Lynch and Nicholas Phillipson
to be identified as the authors of
this work has been asserted in
accordance with the Copyright,
Designs and Patent Act 1988.

Grateful acknowledgement is made for
permission to reproduce material
previously published elsewhere. Every
effort has been made to trace the
copyright holders, but if any have been
inadvertently overlooked, the publisher
will be pleased to make the necessary
arrangements at the first opportunity.

Frontispiece: The Quadrangle, Old
College. Photograph by Edwin Smith,
from Youngson, *The Making of
Classical Edinburgh*

CONTENTS

FOREWORD

In 2003 the University of Edinburgh has around 21,000 students, 7,000 staff and 400 buildings. Most of us who learn, teach or research in this great institution find it quite hard to get to know and understand the particular academic school or administrative division we belong to. The idea of coming to grips with the history of the entire University is quite daunting. This wonderful short book captures the full sweep of our extraordinary history in limpid prose that carries the reader through the 421 years since our enabling charter was granted. It is written by three very distinguished historians who deal in turn with the creation of the university, its key role in the enlightenment and its evolution into one of the world's major universities. Part of the University's distinctiveness came from its intimate relationship with the evolving city and also from its position as Britain's first post-Reformation University. Another key to understanding the University is the way that, with the Royal Colleges in Edinburgh, it invented the modern medical school. The book describes brilliantly the individuals and intellectual movements that contributed to the University's successes and the way the University came to be used as an inspirational model around the world for new civic universities and for new medical schools. I was especially fascinated by the accounts of how the successes of overseas universities, particularly Leiden and other Dutch universities, influenced the development of our University. The University has always had a wonderful tradition of collecting portraits, pictures and objects associated with its history. The fine illustrations in this book go very well with the vivid prose that brings to life past generations of students and an astonishing sequence of distinguished professors.

TIMOTHY O'SHEA,

PRINCIPAL

PREFACE

Edinburgh University has not been particularly well served by historians. The last full-length history, Sir Alexander Grant's *Story of the University of Edinburgh*, was published in 1884 as part of the university's tercentennial celebrations. A later project for a new full-length history resulted in D. B. Horn's excellent *A Short History of the University of Edinburgh, 1556–1889*, which was published in 1967, but lacked what Horn called the third act which would have brought it up to date. Since then the university has attracted a fair amount of attention from historians of the Scottish Enlightenment and from historians interested in university history. However, it still lacks the authoritative, archivally based history it so badly needs and so richly deserves.

This short history is a modest attempt by three Edinburgh historians to view the university's history with modern eyes. We decided to leave it to others to write about its Regents and Professors and their contributions to learning. We have resisted the temptation of telling the university's story in evolutionary terms. We have tried to see how the university responded to the political, religious, economic, social and cultural pressures to which it has been subjected throughout the ages, and we have been mindful of the fact that, historically, the primary duty of any university in any age has been to prepare young men and, more recently, young women for public and professional life. Universities have always prided themselves on being havens of academic freedom. Readers of the present volume may be surprised to learn that, in the course of its long history, no university could have been more responsive, and often more egregiously responsive, to external religious and political pressures than ours. There is probably a moral there.

This, then, does not claim to be an authoritative history. We have each drawn on our own scholarly resources and on some excellent specialist research carried out by others in the past generation. We have tried to bring general readers up to date with current thinking and we have tried to write a book which will stimulate scholarly interest in a sadly neglected subject.

In conclusion, we would like to thank those without whose help this project would have proved impossible: Arnott Wilson, the University Archivist; Margaret Stewart, who created a visual archive of materials; Richard Ovenden, Keeper of Special Collections; our editor, John Davey; and Jackie Jones, Editorial Director of Edinburgh University Press. For three years the university supported a postgraduate programme on the history of the university, and we have benefited from the archival discoveries and theses of the students who participated – Niall Stuart, Clive Fenton, John Brady, Kelly Walker and Pieter Dhondt. We are also grateful to Frances Dow, then Dean of the Faculty of Arts, for her support of this initiative. The last word must go to Dr Martin Lowe, late Secretary to the university, for encouraging this project from the start and for making it viable.

MICHAEL LYNCH, NICHOLAS PHILLIPSON, ROBERT D. ANDERSON

PART I

The Creation of a College

Michael Lynch

Edinburgh's 'tounis college' first opened its doors to students on 10 October 1583. It was Scotland's first institution of higher learning to be founded after the Reformation. It was located in a town that had a rapidly growing population and that was in the process of remaking itself as a capital city, the centre of the royal court, government and administration, in addition to its accustomed role as a merchants' burgh and market town. Some 14,000 people lived in the royal burgh in the 1580s, but nearby Canongate and the two ports of Leith, plus a transient population of nobles, courtiers, crown *fonctionnaires*, lawyers, traders and hucksters added at least half as much again to the population. From 1579 onwards the royal court, with a basic household some 450 strong, was in near-permanent residence at Holyrood. Increasingly, as the tentacles of government reached out more regularly and persistently into the localities during the personal reign of James VI (1567–1625), more and more roads led to the capital. Meetings of parliament, the Convention of Royal Burghs and the General Assembly all now took place, almost invariably, in Edinburgh, which was also the seat of the increasingly centralised courts of both criminal and civil law. Courtiers, lawyers and lobbyists jostled for favour and status in a town that was becoming more and more overcrowded, expensive to live in and violent in its streets.

A university could be an affliction as well as an asset. Throughout most of western Europe students had, since the Middle Ages, developed an unenviable reputation for drunkenness, brawling and whoring. Worse, universities were founded by bishops, and both staff and students might also enjoy legal and social privileges, granted to them by their ecclesiatical patrons, setting them apart from local society. Medieval Brussels, Barcelona and sixteenth-century Nuremberg had all turned down the prospect of a university on these grounds. This may be why the Edinburgh town council was intent, from the outset, to exercise control over an institution which was of its own making and also determined, somewhat less successfully, to have the students live within the college's precincts, under a strictly regulated regime.

Yet in another sense, this hardly seems to be a question worth posing. The need for a 'greater school' was part of the 'make-over' by which Edinburgh was grooming itself as the new capital of a modern, more centralised state, a process which accelerated in the 1580s and 1590s, after the young king came of age and settled into near-permanent residence at Holyrood. The point is often made that the new college was needed by the church to provide it with ministers; 103 of the 259 graduates of the first ten years, or just under 40 per cent, went into the ministry, but this was at a time when there were mass vacancies in Scotland's 1,100 parishes. In the first four decades of the seventeenth century, when on average there would have been only about forty vacancies a year in the whole of the Scottish church, the proportion of Edinburgh graduates going into the ministry fell to one in five. By then, if not before, it was clear that the new state needed well-educated bureaucrats in greater numbers than the new church needed clergy.

In a wider context, the creation of Edinburgh's new college can be seen as part of an expansion of higher education throughout northern Europe, which had marked the period since 1450 and, more specifically, as part of an accelerating wave in the last quarter of the sixteenth century, the result of rival Protestant and Counter-Reformation educational offensives. Protestant (and mostly Calvinist) institutions founded in the same period included Leiden (1575), Helmstedt (1575/6), Orthez (upgraded from an academy to a university in 1583), Franeker (1585), Trinity College, Dublin (1592), Marischal College, Aberdeen (1593), and the Huguenot academies at Saumur (1596), Montauban (1598) and Sedan (1599/1602). In a world of bewildering and often sudden change, where mental confusion and social disorder threatened, the idea of a 'commonweal of the educated' brought considerable comfort. Humanist circles, made up of lawyers, leading merchants and crown administrators, are known to have existed in Edinburgh in the generation in which the first plans for a college were

4

laid. The so-called Bannatyne circle, a group of educated *literati* recorded by the Edinburgh-based scribe George Bannatyne in the 1560s, was notable for two interlocking agendas: a patriotic and conservative instinct to preserve the common treasury of the past; and an Erasmian or Christian humanist objective which stressed the need not only to preserve existing knowledge but also to explore and extend it to arrive at a more authentic truth.

Another set of motives is likely to have involved a combination of civic pride and economic calculation. Each of Scotland's existing universities was set in the closeted atmosphere of a bishop's burgh. Edinburgh's college, by contrast, was to be in a busy metropolis. Here, there may have been some sense of promoting a civic version of the new idea of the commonweal which had emerged in Scotland in the 1530s. Towns were widely seen, not least by Protestant reformers, as the potential growth-points of both a reformation of religion and a reformation of manners. In taking on the role of 'civiliser', the burgh was implicitly challenging the existing, natural leadership of society. The royal burgh, which in a strict sense had long been as much a 'chief vassal' of the crown as any aristocrat, was now claiming the intellectual high ground, rivalling a noble view of culture and chivalry which predominated in both the royal court and the households of the landed classes. The community of the burgh, or at least the various circles within its educated elite, was staking a claim to make a greater contribution than before to the wider community of the realm. A new vogue for civic improvement meshed with a wider-based notion of 'civility', embraced not least by James VI, who saw a spoonful of education as the cure for 'barbarity'.

One further, less idealistic motive undoubtedly existed. As the Presbyterian historian David Calderwood sourly complained, minding 'their particular' was the 'religion of Edinburgh'. A local college, with differential rates for local and other students, would be a far cheaper option for Edinburgh parents than sending their sons elsewhere. But it was also a more reassuring prospect than dispatching children, still on average aged only fourteen or so (though some, more gifted boys were as young as twelve), from the privileged confines of the local grammar school to the rough and rowdy environment of a university town.

Much of this is surmised since the town college, unfortunately, has no surviving constitution (as have, for example, Aberdeen's two university colleges set up in 1495 and 1593) to help explain. Yet neither of Aberdeen's rationales seems to fit the distinctive case of Edinburgh. In 1495 Bishop William Elphinstone claimed that his creation, located in the bishop's burgh of Old Aberdeen, would bring civility to a local population that was 'rude and ignorant of letters, almost barbarous'. And a century later, the Earl Marischal, in tandem with the town council of New Aberdeen, virtually replicated this curriculum and constitution to create another college, which seems to have had the ambition to become a better Protestant seminary than its rival. The aims of the key players in the creation of Edinburgh's college, a dozen years before Marischal College emerged, seem confused and sometimes self-contradictory. Was it intended to be a college devoted to the study of the liberal arts or a Protestant seminary, designed to produce much-needed recruits for the parish ministry? Was it to be a new-style college or an old-style university? Was it to be a college for the town or an institution meant to attract students from afar? The irony is that the scheme was, at one time or another in its pre-history, all of these things. And the dilemmas which studded the years before its foundation remained for a considerable time after it had been created.

The story of the origins of Edinburgh's 'tounis college' has a number of different beginnings. The earliest two belong to the second half of the 1550s. One concerns the provision made by Robert Reid, Bishop of Orkney, in his will for the education of his wayward nephew, Walter Reid, Abbot of Kinloss. It envisaged the creation of three schools – for basic grammar, the arts (based on rhetoric and poetry) and canon and civil law – within a single college. The bequest was lost sight of in the turbulent years which followed his death in 1558, which brought religious change, schism, purges and violence to the burgh. The other strand belongs to the appointments of 'royal lecturers' made by Mary of Guise in 1556. This initiative, which replicated similar appointments made in the Collège de France in Paris, underlined two points. It showed that there was already a pool of talent within the burgh, especially in the key humanist areas of learning and the law. One of these lecturers, who was appointed to give three public lectures a week in law and Greek, was Edward Henryson, who had both studied and taught at Bourges and was qualified in civil law; he would re-emerge at a later, key point in the long story of the college's pre-history, in 1579. The initiative taken by the Queen Regent also underscored the need for government intervention to bring the burgh's ambitions for a college to fruition. It would not and did not materialise until the privy council issued what is usually termed an enabling charter in 1582.

The Protestant reformers who composed the 'Book of Reformation' (usually now known as the *First Book of Discipline*), in 1560, devoted more space in it to education than to any other subject. But the committee that wrote it was an uneasy coalition of reformers and schoolmen: the 'six Johns', as they are sometimes called, included the firebrand John Knox, who had been appointed first minister of Edinburgh in 1559, and two academics from St Andrews, Winram and Douglas, who had been very late converts to the new religion and were anxious to preserve their own institution's place as the senior among the 'great schools' or universities. Edinburgh had ambitions to oust St Andrews from its position as a 'mirrour and exampill to the whole realm' but the 1560s were hardly the time to bring ambitious and costly projects into being in the capital. Knox himself would have been suspicious of any scheme to bring into his own parish what he called the 'bondage of the universities'. And the Reformation crisis of 1559–60 had produced a period of real instability in the capital which persisted for much of the following decade. The existing town council had been forcibly purged of its Catholics and conservatives by the Protestant Lords of the Congregation

when they entered the town in 1559 and a replacement regime made up of zealots and obscure men put in its place; it came under growing pressure from the weight of moderate opinion in the burgh. There were difficulties even meeting existing commitments (including Knox's stipend) without resort to new, unpopular taxation. Recurrently, the capital found itself in the cockpit of further political crises which were not of its making, ranging from the murder of David Rizzio, Savoyard servant of Mary, Queen of Scots in 1566, to a civil war that lasted the better part of five years from 1568 onwards, with Edinburgh as its focal point. As more settled conditions set in after the end of the war in 1573, and Edinburgh was able to recover from the financial ravages of being a battlefield between the rival Queen's and King's parties, the idea of a college of higher learning began to take shape again.

One of the main proponents of the scheme was James Lawson, who had succeeded Knox as first minister of the burgh after Knox's death in 1572. Lawson was out of a different mould from Knox. A graduate of St Mary's College at St Andrews and a late convert, his early career had been in education rather than the parish ministry: he had been appointed a regent at St Mary's in 1568 and then sub-principal at King's College, Aberdeen, after it was purged in 1569. That post carried with it the job of minister in nearby St Machar's cathedral until he succeeded Knox in Edinburgh. In the later 1570s, he renewed his acquaintance with Andrew Melville, whom he had known as a student at St Mary's in the late 1550s. Melville, who would become the leading figure in the second generation of post-Reformation divines, was now Principal of the University of Glasgow and the architect of a new regime at St Mary's, which would be put in place when he was appointed as its Principal in 1580. The new arrangements affected both what was taught and how it was taught. Theology, history and geography were given a place in the curriculum and the system of regenting was swept way in favour of more specialist teaching. Lawson, who has been described by a previous historian of Edinburgh University as the 'chief promoter' of the scheme for

The title page of Theodore Beza's *Icones* (1580), celebrating the young scholar king, James VI, who is portrayed as a royal patron of Protestantism, holding a drawn sword and an olive branch – symbols of war and peace. (Edinburgh University Library, Special Collections)

a town college, envisaged a divinity school like St Mary's, also known at the time as an 'anti-seminary', since its key purpose was to resist the challenge of the Catholic university seminaries that threatened to swamp Scotland with missionary priests and Jesuits. But Lawson's idea would be lost in the vortex of Edinburgh and national politics of the early 1580s.

On 10 October 1583 the General Assembly of the Church of Scotland, barely a generation old, met in St Giles' in Edinburgh's High Street. The main topic on its agenda, held over from its last two meetings, was the future of Scotland's universities. The moderator was Robert Pont, minister of St Cuthbert's and master of the Trinity College, both just outside Edinburgh's walls, and all four of Edinburgh's ministers were among those chosen to act as the moderator's assessors, drawing up the agenda and resolutions to be considered by the Assembly. Detailed reports on a formal visitation of the universities of Aberdeen, Glasgow and St Andrews were presented, considering the teaching methods, the content of the curriculum and funding. Teaching in grammar schools was discussed as well as that in the 'greater schools'. Yet there were two curious elements about this meeting of the Assembly. One was that part of the debate, or at least the record of it, was conducted in Latin – the first and last time that this was so. It took the form of an ennumerated onslaught on the errors of Aristotelianism in the teaching of philosophy by grammar schoolmasters and university regents alike. The other oddity was that there was no mention in this debate of the momentous event taking place a mere two hundred yards away – the opening of Scotland's first new university since the Reformation. Silence spoke loudly.

The new 'tounis college', as it was called, had a modest beginning in many ways. There was no extensive (and expensive) building programme such as had delayed the opening of King's College, Aberdeen, for over ten years after its formal foundation in 1495. Yet the opening of its doors to its first students in the autumn of 1583, sixteen months after the formal, enabling royal charter to sanction its foundation had been granted (in June 1582), camouflaged an intense struggle which had taken place in both national and burgh politics over the previous two or three years. It is agreed in most accounts that the scheme for a town college, first mooted in the later 1550s, had been revived in 1579, when a committee had been set up by the town council to investigate the feasibility of siting a college on the north-eastern edge of the burgh, close to or in the old Trinity College. These first meetings talked loosely of 'ane universitie' and even, at times, of 'the universities'. By the end of 1579, the debate had narrowed to a rather different prospect – 'ane college of theologe'. The main proponent of this idea was James Lawson. He lived with his fellow ministers 'verie commodiouslie togidder, as in a Collage', according to James Melville, nephew of Andrew. Their lodging, located close by St Giles', was, in a sense, already a theological seminary. This was why it was the natural home for the theological books in the library of Clement Little, a prominent Edinburgh lawyer who died in 1580 and became, almost by accident, the first benefactor of the college.

The scheme hit a number of obstacles, both practical and ideological. A home for the new college proved difficult to find. Edinburgh had reaped very little financial benefit from the break-up of the old church. A large part of the grant made by Queen Mary in 1567 of the lands and rents of the burgh's friaries had evaporated. Money, or the lack of it, would afflict the new college for fully the first half-century of its existence. Trinity College, a seemingly natural home, was still in the hands of its provost – the same man, Robert Pont, who would preside over the Assembly of October 1583. His legal talents – he was a senator of the College of Justice and a canon lawyer as well as a parish minister – served to defend his financial interests. The town council lobbied both crown and parliament to help finance its scheme for a college for over two years, until a royal charter, in the name of James VI, was issued in April 1582.

In the process, however, two rival schemes crystallised, against a background of sharpening political and religious tensions, both at court and in the capital itself. In these years, the former regent, the Earl of Morton, staged a political comeback, fell for a second time and was executed on a trumped-up charge. A new regime, headed by the king's cousin, Esmé Stewart, recently arrived from France and deeply distrusted by radical elements within the kirk, took control, until ousted by the so-called Ruthven Raid in the summer of 1582. The Ruthven regime, in turn, collapsed in June 1583 and was replaced by a new administration under the control of the Earl of Arran, who had been Esmé's right-hand man. The interplay of factionalism at court, now based after 1579 almost permanently in the Palace of Holyroodhouse, impacted directly on burgh politics. Rival parties – initially named after Morton and Esmé Stuart – vied for control of the council chamber. By 1582, each had its own distinctive vision of the prospective town college.

Three stages in this complex process of wrangling between rival factions are worth noting. When the enabling charter was granted in April 1582, a 'moderate' party was in power, led by the provost Alexander Clerk, who later confessed, in his own words, to have gone 'courting' to secure it, much to the fury of James Lawson and his fellow ministers. The Ruthven Raid, in

The second page of the college's Laureation Register, dated 1585, takes the form of a subscription to the Confession of Faith and a rant against the evils of popery. A test act on office-holders had become mandatory in 1572 and this version is dependent on the King's Confession (later dubbed the Negative Confession), subscribed by the young King James and his court in 1581. (Edinburgh University Library, Special Collections) turn, was hailed by Lawson and others in the General Assembly as an 'act of reformation'. The real convictions of the Ruthven regime probably did not live up to this accolade, but what is relevant to the story of the town college is that the practical arrangements made to bring it into being were mostly drawn up and carried through in the twelve months prior to its opening by a radical faction in the town council, brought to power at the elections of Michaelmas 1582; it was sympathetic to the Ruthvenites and backed by the town's ministers. It was during its term of office that masters of work were appointed (in December 1582), a tax was levied on the burgh to pay for the work (in June 1583), and the college's first member of staff was appointed (in September), following a full-scale debate in the council chamber to discuss the merits of the candidates. The choice of Robert Rollock seems to have been made largely on the recommendation of James Lawson, although he seems not personally to have known this son of a Stirlingshire laird – a graduate of St Andrews, who had teaching experience as a regent at St Salvator's.

The story, however, had another, final twist. In June 1583, the Ruthven regime collapsed. It had come to power, ten months before, by seizing the person of the young king; it lost power by the equally sure method of allowing him to escape. A full-scale reaction set in, against both its members and its fellow travellers, who included Edinburgh's town council and its radical ministers. With its days in power clearly numbered, the council was gripped by a desperate sense of urgency in the autumn of 1583. It strove to bring the building work and other arrangements to completion before the term was due to begin – as it always has since (at least until the onset of 'semesters' in 2004) – in the opening week of October. The next burgh election, however, also took place in the same week and the new council proved to be a very different body from the one which it replaced. Two leets were produced, in the name of the king, nominating more than half of the council and all its office-bearers. This was as large a change as at any election since the crisis year of 1559, when the Protestant Lords of the Congreg-

ation had invaded the burgh and swept away a loyalist town council. The coup brought to power a faction closely allied to the court and determined to wash its hands of its troublesome ministers and most of their works, including their vision for the town college. It was hardly likely to endorse plans to make the capital's college another seminary, like that of Andrew Melville at St Mary's, designed to produce more ministers out of the same radical mould. For his part, James Lawson, from the safety of his self-inflicted exile in London, later described the incomers as 'wolves'.

This was why Edinburgh's town college had such an unusual beginning. Two weeks after it came to power, the new council announced plans to overhaul the arrangements made

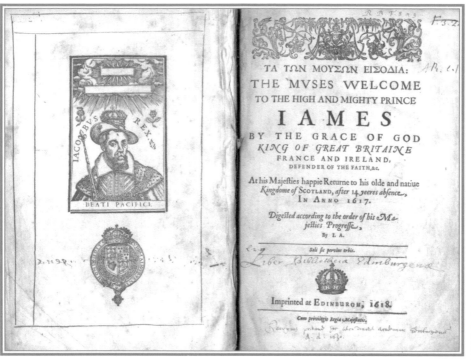

by its predecessor. The result was that the new college came into being with students, one teacher, an impossible staff–student ratio perhaps as heavy as 1:80, makeshift premises but no agreed curriculum. The following twelve months produced further profound changes in both national and burgh politics but only muddle for the college. The so-called Black Acts parliament, which met behind closed doors in the Edinburgh tolbooth in May 1584, with some of the town's troublemakers and their wives excluded from the burgh while it sat, triggered a flight of the burgh's ministers into exile in England, where Lawson died before the end of the year. The crisis of 1584 brought more direct royal control in the capital, over both the town council and the kirk session, and it provoked intense rumours that St Mary's College, Andrew Melville's creation of 1581, which was seen as the nursery of radicalism, was to be closed down. Over the same period, the new Edinburgh curriculum, so hastily redrawn during the first month of the college's existence, had to be rethought. The compromise it represented came apart, for it overlapped sub-

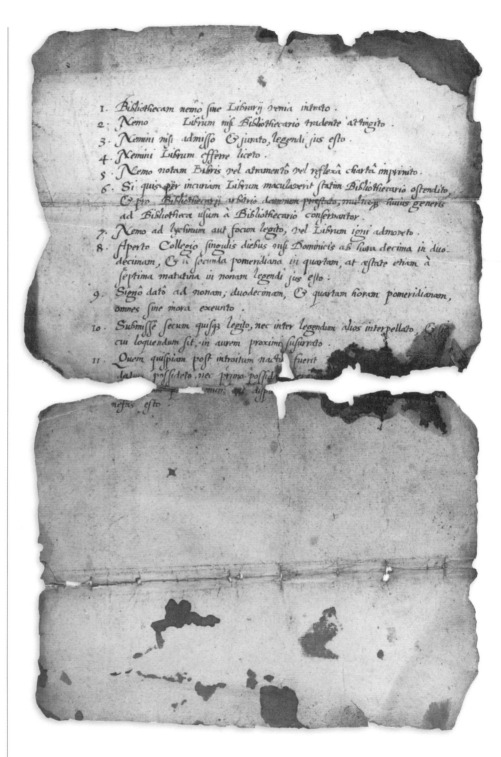

1. Bibliothecam nemo sine Librarij venia intrato.
2. Nemo   Librum nisi Bibliothecario tradente attingito.
3. Nemini nisi admisso & jurato, legendi jus esto.
4. Nemini Librum efferre liceto.
5. Nemo notam Libris vel atramento vel reflexa charta imprimito.
6. Si quis per incuriam Librum maculaverit statim Bibliothecario ostendito
   & pro Bibliothecarij arbitrio damnum prestato; multisque huius generis
   ad Bibliotheca usum à Bibliothecario conservantor.
7. Nemo ad lychnum aut focum legito, vel Librum igni admoveto.
8. Aperto Collegio singulis diebus nisi Dominicis ab hora decima in duodecimam, & à secunda pomeridiana in quartam, at aestate etiam à
   septima matutina in nonam legendi jus esto:
9. Signo dato ad nonam; duodecimam, & quartam horam pomeridianam,
   omnes sine mora exeunto.
10. Submisse secum quisq; legito, nec inter legendum alios interpellato, &
    cu loquendum sit, in aurem proximi susurrato.
11. Quem quispiam post introitum nactus fuerit
    locum possideto, nec primo possid...
    nefas esto.

A page from a book, *Athanae bataviae* (Leiden, 1625), donated to the library in 1641 by David McCall, Edinburgh merchant and town councillor. Although the layout of the college's library is unknown, its classification system, revealed in its first catalogue of 1636, probably closely followed that in the library of the University of Leiden, illustrated here. (Edinburgh University Library, Special Collections)

stantially with the curriculum taught in the burgh's own grammar school. The boundaries between what was taught in the college and grammar school had to be reviewed yet again in the autumn of 1584, following the appointment of a new master of the latter, Hercules Rollock, who seems to have overhauled its curriculum. At the same time, taking advantage of the absence of its exiled ministers, the council seized the opportunity to move Clement Little's library out of the ministers' lodging and into the college at the Kirk o' Field, redesignating it in the process the 'townis librarie'. Another skeleton in the closet of the new institution was created in the process.

Despite its eccentricities, the up-and-down story of the foundation and opening of the Edinburgh college in the early and mid-1580s set down patterns which would dominate its history for some time to come. First, the college was from its outset – and before – subject to close scrutiny and supervision by the town council. Second, it was badly short of proper financing and would remain so until at least the 1630s, for it

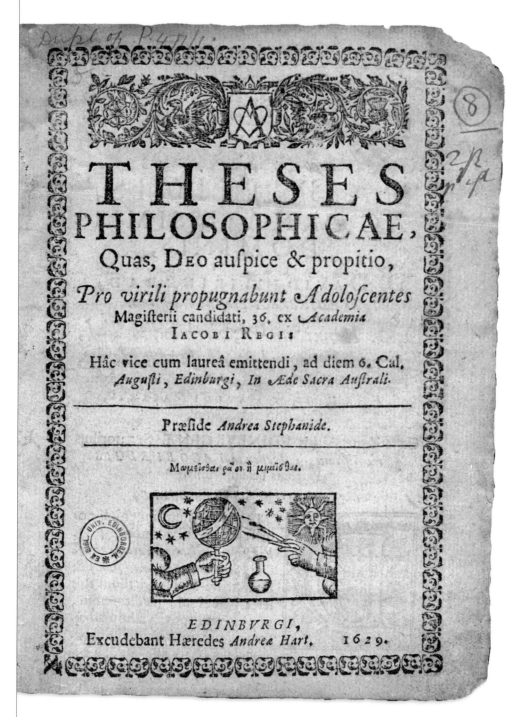

THESES
PHILOSOPHICAE,
Quas, Deo auspice & propitio,

Pro virili propugnabunt Adoloscentes
Magisterii candidati, 36. ex *Academia*
Iacobi Regis:

Hâc vice cum laureâ emittendi, ad diem 6. Cal.
Augusti, Edinburgi, In Æde Sacra Australi.

Præside *Andrea Stephanide.*

Μωμεῖσθαι ῥᾷον ἢ μιμεῖσθαι.

EDINBVRGI,
Excudebant Hæredes *Andreæ Hart.* 1629.

was only then that private charity began to emerge in sums large enough to make up for a recurrent shortfall from public sources. It had become a habit for Edinburgh authorities to add – with the so-called 'eke' – to what was becoming regularly levied national taxes in order to pay for its local projects. In March 1585, in an unprecedented level of 'eke', the council tripled a national tax to help pay for building work on the college and St Giles'. Taxation on this scale and frequency was unpopular and must have strained the enthusiasm of many for the 'tounis college'. But another effect of the expenditure on capital works was strikingly low levels of stipend for teaching staff. The second regent to be appointed, Duncan Nairn, in November 1583, was paid a mere 40 merks (£27) a year plus board, the same rate of pay as that of a reader, on the lowliest rung of the parish ministry. A glimpse of the council's priorities may be gleaned from the fact that the master of works to the college, a sinecure created for an elderly merchant and ex-councillor, was paid 100 merks, more than twice as much as Duncan Nairn. One inevitable result which recurred with some frequency throughout the first century of the town college's life was a high turnover of teaching staff, as they left to take up better-paid jobs as parish ministers. One of the town's own ministers claimed in 1586 that a single man in the ministry needed a minimum of 300 merks (£200) a year to live on, while a minister with wife and family could scarcely live on 400 merks. This may have been why Rollock had his salary as principal increased to that figure in 1587, although he had also to agree to act as a locum and unpaid preacher in one of the burgh's four parishes as part of the arrangement. For others, however, university teaching was a job for the young, the underpaid or the confirmed bachelor.

Third, from the beginning the fortunes of the college were closely tied to the warmth or otherwise of the relationship between capital and court. In the early years, the college benefited from the calculated fawning of the court party in burgh politics. The council turned to the Earl of Arran, the provost peremptorily imposed upon it by the crown in 1584, to solve its problems over the ownership of Trinity College. As a result, it benefited from the acquisition of the revenues of both the vicarage of Currie and Paisley Abbey, although both produced less than had been anticipated, and it also managed to bring the wrangling with Pont over Trinity College to a more or less satisfactory conclusion. But there may have been a price to pay for royal favour. One of the most prominent of the supporters of the revised college scheme in 1581–2 was Patrick Adamson, Archbishop of St Andrews and Chancellor of its university. A bitter enemy of Andrew Melville, his troublesome colleague based in St Mary's, Adamson seized the opportunity to encourage a project which at that point was so firmly associated with critics of radical Presbyteranism. It does seem unlikely, however, that Adamson would have let his political instincts run away with his proprietorial interests as chancellor of a rival university. It may be that some tacit arrangement was arrived at, as was later explictly agreed in 1616, when Edinburgh's students were restricted (at least in theory) to 'bernis of thair awne city'. Whatever the motives of Adamson, there can be no doubt, unpalatable as it may have been to many, that the town college was the creature not of radical presbyterianism, but of the young scholar-king, James VI, and his court, and of the new understanding being forged in the early 1580s between it and the capital.

What was taught and how was it taught? These are obvious but awkward questions which cannot be answered with any certainty. One school of thought stoutly maintains that the new curriculum was cast in the same mould as that of Andrew Melville's at St Mary's, influenced by the work of Pierre de La Ramée, or Peter Ramus in the more often used Latinised form of his name. Ramist thought, an assault on the Aristotelian and scholastic traditions of logic and philosophy, is usually taken as a hallmark of radical Presbyterianism, and indeed the radical council of 1582–3 used the form 'academia', one of the watchwords of Ramism, to signal its intent. This suggested a more rigorous and innovative curriculum than that implied in the foundation charter of earlier in 1582 or that which Rollock actually put into operation when he took up his post in October 1583. The circumstances of Rollock's appointment and his early teaching career at St Salvator's, a stronghold of traditional Aristotelian philosophy and of anti-Ramist thought under its principal, John Rutherford, do not suggest that he was an innovator, either in the curriculum or in teaching methods. And the political circumstances of the first years after the college's foundation point in the same direction. In December 1584, the provost and bailies are recorded as making a visitation to the college to oversee 'the lessons made there'. It seems unthinkable that the town council, with the Earl of Arran, a nominee of the crown as its provost, would approve a curriculum promoted by Andrew Melville, who at that moment was in exile in England and his own college of St Mary's closed.

It has been said by one recent commentator that 'the craze for Ramism was out of all proportion to the insights Ramus had to offer'. Whether the craze for Ramism belonged to later sixteenth-century academics or to modern-day historians, who have tried to wedge the Edinburgh case into larger patterns linking Ramism with religious and political radicalism, is a moot point. Undoubtedly Ramist thought profoundly influenced both the curriculum and teaching practice at Melville's two institutions – the University of Glasgow and St Mary's College. It was introduced in a more diluted form at Marischal College, where regenting (the system in which one tutor taught a class all subjects throughout its four years of study) persisted. At Edinburgh, the difficulty is that the evidence comes late. The curriculum is first fully described in college statutes drawn up in 1628, *Disciplia academiae Edinburgenae … prout observata sunt multis retro annis.* The problem lies in divining how many years some of the practices which it describes had been in operation. Much of it seems to have been drawn up as a result of ongoing discussions between 1619 and 1628. The fact that the 1628 statute contains both Ramist logic and some specialisation did not have the same significance in 1628 as it would have had in the 1580s. By then, the sting had gone out of Ramism, and its main use had become a means of inculcating logic into reluctant or dim-witted students by providing a methodical analysis of a subject, breaking it down into its component parts and a series of contraries – the early-modern equivalent of the multi-choice test. The radical new wave of supposedly innovative teaching of the 1570s and 1580s had become little more than a convenient blunt instrument for harassed teachers.

A second piece of evidence is more persuasive. John Adamson, son of the provost of Perth and a graduate from Edinburgh in 1597, wrote a life of Charles Ferme, his regent, who had himself been a student in the first class of 1583–7. Adamson claimed that Ferme, 'under Rollock's guidance', had studied 'Greek grammar and the Greek authors, the *Dialecticae* of Ramus' and the rhetoric of Talon, one of the key disciples of Ramus, along with some arithmetic and geography. There are two points to make here. First, there are some resemblances between this curriculum and that which operated in 1628, by which time Adamson was Principal. But, second, when was it first taught? What is described by Adamson is mostly the content of the last two years of the curriculum. In short, it seems likely that this was what Ferme was taught from 1586 onwards, *after* the break in his studies forced by an outbreak of the plague, which stopped all teaching between May 1585 and February 1586. By then, the political complexion of both the burgh and court politics had drastically changed. Arran had been ousted in November 1585, the exiles (Melville among them) had returned, and there had been something of a *rapprochement* between the radical ministers and the king. A diluted Ramist programme of study would not by then have seemed to pose as great a threat as it had in 1583. But diluted it certainly was, not least in three of its central features – regenting, a lack of specialist subjects and a curriculum grounded in the liberal arts rather than in theology, as was the case at St Mary's. The old system, by which one tutor taught a class through all four years of its studies, had, however, one enormous advantage. It was cheaper than any of the new methodologies. It remained in force until the eighteenth century.

Rollock was paid, when first appointed, just £40 per annum plus students' fees. Then as now, students from further afield were more lucrative: the children of townsfolk paid £2 a year and all others £3. It has been guessed that this may have realised him a total wage of about £190. Even so, this was modest and compared badly with the stipend of a minister in an urban parish. When he was appointed Principal in 1586, his salary was increased to 400 merks, with fees on top. But as has been seen, Duncan Nairn, when appointed second master in 1583, received only 40 merks. There may well have been difficulty in finding suitably qualified men at this pittance, which was less than the wage of an average craftsman, for regents by the 1590s were earning £100 per annum, according to Thomas Craufurd, who taught in the college from 1626 onwards. Even so, a distinct impression emerges in this period of a large gulf between an underpaid academic workforce, which carried out most of the hard grind of teaching, and a principal, paid more than three times as much, whose workload, involving only the

Bachelor of Divinity (BD) year, which followed on after the four-year degree Master of Arts (MA), was slight in comparison. It is hardly to be wondered why Rollock scarcely had an unpublished thought in the 1590s, when a score of tracts on covenant theology flowed from his pen. He might today have been called a research professor. His colleagues, in contrast, published little or nothing, afflicted as they were by crushing staff–student ratios and intent on finding more lucrative employment elsewhere. The poor scholarly performance of most of its staff would be a problem which afflicted the town college for most of its first century in being, made worse by a series of undistinguished principals after Rollock died in 1599. The value placed on an institution of higher learning lay not in the scholarship of its staff but in its throughput of students at minimal cost and in the moral instruction inculcated into them.

If the numbers of students and the exact nature of the curriculum cannot be determined with any certainty in the early years of the college's history, nor can the precise motives of the Edinburgh establishment in creating the college. In part, the town council undoubtedly wanted to extend its control over all levels of education practised within its jurisdiction. Part of the story of Edinburgh in this period is that the more the town grew, the more hierarchical and paternalistic the burgh authorities became. Within less than a year of the opening of the college, the council tried to give monopoly status to its own grammar school, banning Edinburgh parents from sending their children to any other than the official 'hie school', and its curriculum was revised at the same time to fit in with the changing teaching programme of the college. The duties of the master of the burgh's grammar school were prescribed as teaching youths piety, good manners, doctrine and letters. The ordering is suggestive; the priorities which the council had set for the town college would not have been greatly different.

The figure of forty-seven graduates in 1587 suggests a high level of demand for a university closer to home and less expen-

The letter 'S' in the student notebook of Adam Blackadder (1672). One of a series of grotesque faces drawn within the capital letters, this is a caricature of his regent, James Pillans, who taught in the college from 1644 to 1681. (Edinburgh University Library, Special Collections)

sive than St Andrews, the natural resort up to that point for most students from Edinburgh. But that figure may well conceal a much higher number of entrants to the first class of 1583. An unknown but large number of youths presented themselves for admission on 1 October 1583; Rollock's biographer (his successor as Principal, Henry Charteris) wrote of 'magna multitudo' thronging the hall of Hamilton House. Many proved not to be up to the mark and failed a language test organised by the bailies ten days later. This was the reason why a second master was suddenly appointed in November 1583, to cope with these unexpectedly high numbers and the poor Latin possessed by many of them. The fact that this post was reintroduced in 1597, in the form of a *regens humaniorum literarum* or regent of humanity, to teach Latin and basic Greek grammar, would suggest that a significant proportion of prospective students needed what was in effect a prep school

and were coming from outside the burgh and its strictly regimented grammar school.

A high drop-out rate can be demonstrated in most years after the data for individual classes become available in the 1630s and there are other reasons to suspect that the class of 1583 may have suffered in this way. It had a particularly troubled career. This was the class whose education had been interrupted for nine months in its second year by a severe outbreak of the plague, which had forced the college to close in May 1585. And the figure of thirty recorded in the Register of Laureations for the following year (1588) almost certainly involves some double-counting; it probably includes those who went on after their first degree to take the one-year Bachelor of Divinity to set them on course for a career in the parish ministry. In either event, a staff–student ratio of this dimension would hardly have been conducive to good teaching practice.

After the initial flurry of enthusiasm which brought extraordinarily high figures of graduates in 1587 and 1588 – forty-seven and thirty – the numbers who emerged with degrees consolidated after the first few years. In the 1590s, the average figure was 24.8; in the first decade of the seventeenth century it was 24.9. By the 1610s, the figure had climbed to 30.7 with no fewer than forty-six in 1617, the largest single graduating class since 1587 at Edinburgh and greater than in any other Scottish university to that point. It may well have been this peak figure which prompted complaints from rival institutions and the attempt made in 1616 to limit Edinburgh's intake only to boys from the burgh. In the 1620s, the average remained much the same, at 30.9, despite one very depressed year because of an isolated outbreak of plague in 1624. By the 1630s, the average number of graduates had reached 36.4.

But this is to measure success by counting the numbers who managed to reach the end of the tunnel of four years of study. Student statistics are notoriously unreliable, especially if trends are detached from actual names, as they must be until fuller data become available in the 1670s. Even so, it can be guessed that the model student who arrived as a 'bajan' (now called a 'fresher') and graduated four years later was at times probably in a minority. From the 1630s onwards, the numbers of entrants who matriculated begin to emerge in the record. A comparison of matriculation and graduation statistics produces a very different picture. Drop-out rates were phenomenally high by modern standards, ranging from 21 per cent to 57 per cent in the two decades from 1639 onwards. These, of course, were years of immense disruption, including war, plague, invasion and a Cromwellian military garrison. But the drop-out rates in the 1660s, after the Restoration had brought a measure of political stability, at least in Edinburgh, were higher still: an appalling 64 per cent of the class of 1658 failed to graduate in 1662. The average drop-out figure was well over a third, enough now to bring penal sanctions from government on an offending university.

Closer scrutiny of these figures is possible when the

numbers of students passing into the second-year class – the *supervenientes* or 'semis' – become available from 1670 onwards. The first-year class of 1669 numbered seventy. A year later, only forty-nine survived to move on into a second year of study. The details of *supervenientes* seem to suggest that dropping-out was at its highest in the first year: in 1672–3, only thirty-two out of a first-year class of eighty-five survived into second year and in the next year twenty-six out of fifty-nine. First-year drop-out rates could be as high as 60 per cent. Before adverse comparison are made with modern trends, it needs to be recognised that the study regime of the seventeenth century would appal most of today's students, who now typically face examinations only twice a session, as would the workload and contact hours. The students' day began at 5 a.m. in summer and 6 a.m. in winter – precisely the same hours as those of the rest of the urban workforce. The regime was relaxed by an hour later in the seventeenth century, when students were allowed the luxury of staying in bed until 6 a.m. in summer and 7 a.m. in winter. But class hours spilled over into the weekend: instruction continued on both Saturday and Sunday mornings. The demands of the first-year curriculum, which introduced students to the great authors in Latin and Greek, were relentless: it 'continuallie' involved large amounts of rote learning of grammar, with regular – at times daily – class tests, which steadily turned the screw, first entailing translation from Latin to English and latterly from Latin to Greek or vice versa. Many students must have found such an intensive if basic curriculum intimidating. John Lauder, later Lord Fountainhall, who was a student from 1660 to 1664, recalled in later years that his regent, Mr James Pillans, son of an Edinburgh burgess and another product of the college, was fond of admonishing his students with the missionary statement: 'I think you have forgot ye are *sub ferula* under the rod. Ye must know that I am your Master not only to instruct but to chastise you.' Edinburgh, indeed, seems early on to have developed a reputation as a hard school; in 1611 the town council was forced to appeal to the privy council to prevent students who had failed

Another character drawn by Alexander Wilson during his time in James Pillans' third-year class of 1662–3; it has a heading, 'The profoundest picture of Robert Hall drawn to the life'. The dog Latin epithet on the opposite page, 'Un fucris felix multos memorialis amicos' suggests a student drop-out rather than a scholar in the making. There is no record that he ever finished his degree. (Edinburgh University Library, Special Collections)

their Edinburgh exams from migrating to easier regimes elsewhere.

One of the main reasons for the high drop-out rates may well have been the variable quality of grammar-school education. Successive commissions of the General Assembly from the 1580s onwards tried to impose a more uniform curriculum on all grammar schools and to insist that students should not be allowed to progress from the first year until they had a sound command of Latin. Although no systematic survey of origins is possible, students who went to the Edinburgh college came from a wide arc of Lowland Scotland, from Dumfries in the south-west to Fife and Perthshire. This may be why, from the very beginning, a regent of humanity was needed to brush up the Latin and Greek of applicants before they were allowed to enter their first year of study. It may also explain the increasing trend in the later seventeenth century of *supervenientes anno secundo*, or allowing well-qualified and gifted youths, who had already been put through a strict mill of study at superior grammar schools such as Edinburgh's own, to enter straight into the second-year class. What is now coyly called 'advanced standing' has a long history.

On the other hand, the number of graduates who survived to the end of four years of study at times was greater than the number going into the second-year class. This would seem to suggest a very different pattern of study between seventeenth-century students and their modern counterparts. It is likely that drop-outs dropped back into their studies after a break, during which they presumably mugged up on their Latin and Greek grammar. A clue to how greatly needed this could be comes from a modern commentator who examined the Latin verses composed by beginners at the college: 'the Latin varies from the incompetent to the perplexing'. Quite how such under-performers might have survived the formal, public *disputatio* in their final year is equally perplexing, if, of course, they survived till then. The number of private teachers in Edinburgh recorded in the poll tax of the 1690s – as well as the strictures of both the General Assembly and college authorities – suggest that there was a booming industry in coaching the reluctant or the dim up to an acceptable standard of proficiency in the classical languages.

Another variant which may help explain the drop-out or failure rates lies with the standard of care exercised by college regents, who taught the same students in all four years of their studies. There are visible, at times, significant variations in the

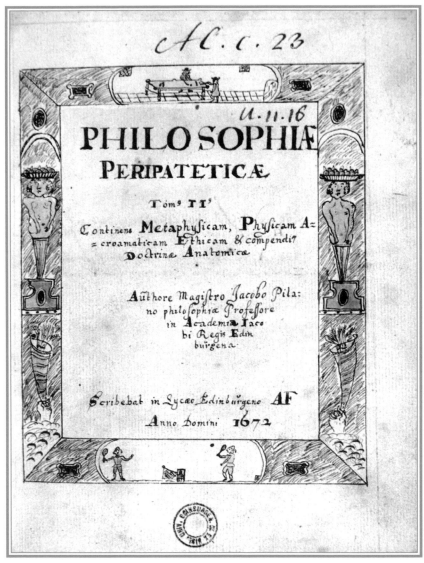

PHILOSOPHIÆ PERIPATETICÆ.

Tóm⁹ II⁹

Continens Metaphyſicam, Phyſicam Az=croamaticam Ethicam & compendiꝰ Doctrinæ Anatomicæ

Authore Magiſtro Jacobo Pila:no philoſophiæ Profeſſore in Academiæ Jacobi Regis Edinburgena.

Scribebat in Lycæo Edinburgeno AF Anno Domini 1672

The title page of Archibald Flint's dictates of James Pillans' lectures (1672), showing his other interests – tennis and billiards. (Edinburgh University Library, Special Collections)

proportion that a regent was able to present for graduation from his original class. It may well be that the most talented scholar was not always the most gifted teacher. Robert Sibbald, future geographer royal and founder member of the Royal College of Physicians, who studied at the college from 1655 to 1659, had a particularly unfortunate undergraduate career: his first two regents died in post and the third, William Tweedie, an Edinburgh graduate who had almost twenty years' experience as a regent at both the town college and St Andrews, gave many in his class (so Sibbald claimed in his *Memoirs*) 'a disgust of him'

THE UNIVERSITY
OF EDINBURGH

32

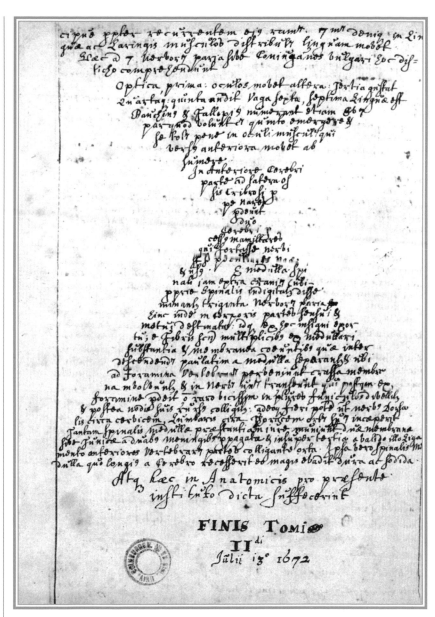

by routinely dictating notes on Aristotle's paraphrases, doubt-
less of many years' standing. Forty-five graduated in that class
of 1655–9 out of an initial entry of sixty-five. By contrast, the
class of the year before it, which had studied in 1654–8 during
the more settled years of the Cromwellian occupation with
Thomas Crauford as its regent, had, on the face of it, a 100 per
cent survival rate, though it is very unlikely that the sixty-five
who graduated in 1658 were precisely the same body of

students who had entered four years earlier. Here, almost certainly, 'drop-ins' are hidden within the statistics as well as drop-outs. Yet Crauford should not be seen as a model teacher: his classes that laureated in 1646, 1650 and 1662 had drop-out rates of 54 per cent, 50 per cent and a phenomenal 64 per cent respectively.

Two other factors must have been at work to explain the striking rise in failure rates. Here, one difficulty is that there is little basis of comparison before the crisis years of the 1640s and 1650s, which brought war, forced taxation, plague (in 1645–6), a sharply declining economy and, from 1651 onwards, military occupation. In 1639–40, which are the first years when a comparison can be made of the numbers in the same class matriculating and graduating, two out of every three 'bajans' survived to laureate. With students who entered the college in the years after 1644, drop-out rates ranged from 46 to 63 per cent. Perhaps surprisingly, the years after the Restoration of 1660 did not see much of an improvement: only two of the six classes which laureated between 1663 and 1668 showed a drop-out rate of under 42 per cent.

A more straightforward reason for the steepening rise in drop-outs in the Restoration period may lie in a more obvious fact – worsening staff–student ratios. It is likely that the numbers of students entering the first-year class were three or even four times as many by the 1680s as at the beginning of the century. This can be demonstrated with certainty after initial matriculation statistics become available from 1639 onwards. Numbers of entrants fluctuated wildly in the 1640s and 1650s but the average size of the first-year class was about sixty. In the first half of the 1660s, it was ninety-three. Some classes later in the same decade were over a hundred in number, but were still taught by one regent. This is to be compared, allowing for exaggeration, with the situation during the career of Thomas Craufurd, the first historian of the university, who taught as a regent between 1626 and 1646. Total numbers, he claimed, presumably counting all four years and the BD class as well, often reached 'sixteen score', suggesting a maximum class size of about sixty. Two conclusions suggest themselves: there was rising demand for student places after the Restoration and the college was failing to expand its staff or to adapt their teaching methods to cope with increased numbers. There may have been a backlash against the rising numbers and falling standards of pastoral care after c. 1670: the average number of entrants fell to fifty-seven a year in the 1670s and fifty-six in the following decade. In some years, the number dropped below forty. Yet these were years in which there was no outbreak of plague or serious political crisis to choke off numbers. It seems more likely that either students voted with their feet and went elsewhere or parents were becoming less willing to indulge in such a speculative investment as four years of formal education of a son in *studium generale*, especially in a town where the cost of living was dramatically rising.

Another possibility is that the mushrooming of private, specialist schools teaching languages, mathematics, navigational skills and other practical subjects had begun to cream off those for whom the seventeenth-century version of the medieval *studium generale* was an affliction rather than the route to a career in the professions. By now, Edinburgh presented a new variety of career options for its sons. The city was a metropolis in the process of becoming gentrified and developing a service sector that already was outgrowing the traditional mainstays of its economy, which had for almost three centuries lain in the export and import trades. By the 1690s, the wealth of its lawyers was greater than that of all its merchants and craftsmen put together; new services were replacing old industries; and there was a flight of the poorer sections of the population to the suburbs to escape higher levels of taxation. In the 1680s and 1690s (as would be the case three centuries later), students brought their own inflationary pressures with them: rents as well as prices were rising sharply. Edinburgh was by now no longer a merchants' town but a professionals' metropolis.

The wider significance of the rise in student numbers at Scotland's universities and colleges in the early seventeenth century has hardly begun to be assessed. In England, large claims have been made, notably by Lawrence Stone, of an 'educational revolution', which began in the 1570s and 1580s and reached a climax in the 1630s, when some 2,000 or so students entered higher education each year. The number graduating MA at Oxford went up by 70 per cent in this period and the number emerging with a BD degree trebled. The difficulty here is, to adapt the wording of a notorious exchange between rival historians of the same period of English history, that the counting of students is at times rather like the counting of sheep and it can have the same hallucinatory effects. At Cambridge, about 4,900 students matriculated in both the 1620s and the 1630s. In Scotland as a whole, taking all seven university colleges (three at St Andrews and two in Aberdeen), the figure for the 1620s is in the region of 1,667. Whether measured against Cambridge numbers or against English figures as a whole, this is a creditable showing. In the period between the 1560s and the 1620s, Scotland's overall student population had increased fivefold. Contemporary 'guestimates' of the relative populations of the two countries put Scotland's at between a tenth or a twelfth of that of England. Thus the collated Scottish figures represent almost exactly one twelfth of those of Stone. If there was a 'revolution' in the provision of higher education in England during this period, a fair case can be made for Scotland experiencing something of the same. Furthermore, Edinburgh in these years consistently provided about one in five of the total of matriculated students.

Here, however, any meaningful comparisons end. In Cambridge, some 35 per cent of the total university population was made up of fellows or officers of the university, giving staff–student ratios in its various colleges which typically stood at less than 1:2. Private charity and benefactions at both Oxford and Cambridge were on a scale unimagined in any of the Scottish institutions, despite some increase in charity at Edinburgh in the 1620s and 1630s. The real difference between the two countries lay not so much in the proportionate numbers of students in society entering higher education as in endowment, library provision, the numbers of teachers and their pay and conditions, and a massive contrast in staff–student ratios.

Each of these points can readily be demonstrated. Cambridge had over 1,000 fellows and officers of the university. Even its most modest college had a larger complement of staff than the six or seven who comprised the teaching force of the Edinburgh town college for much of the first century of its existence. It is difficult for today's university teachers – since the heaviest staff–student ratio in the old Faculty of Arts before its demise in 2002 was the 1:24 in the Department of History – to imagine workloads which were, minimally, twice as great as this and, by the third quarter of the seventeenth century, almost four times as bad. It is unfortunate that none of the reactions of the privileged fellows of the University of Oxford, where the one-to-one tutorial persists to this day, were recorded when they accompanied James VI and I to Edinburgh in 1617, when they met some of their fellow academics. Pay improved over the course of the first century of the college's existence but never matched either the stipend to be earned in a good parish or the fee paid by aristocrats who poached well-qualified regents to act as private tutors to their sons. An alternative to this for the well-heeled was to pay more than the going rate as a fee to their son's regent, as was the case with Sir John Foulis of Ravelston, who gave between £20 and £30 a year, no doubt in the expectation of preferential treatment. That was probably the salvation for many tutors, given the extreme fluctuations in the numbers of entrants which marked the Restoration period. The average number of entrants in the ten-year period of 1668–77 was sixty-five. But this tells nothing for the sequence was as follows: 122, seventy, forty-three, seventy-two, eighty-five, fifty-nine, thirty-eight, eighty-four, forty-four and thirty-five. These deviations must have been particularly bewildering for James Pillans, the regent who took on successive classes in this period of 122, eighty-five and thirty-five. At least his last year in a career which stretched back to 1644 was less taxing than usual; he retired in 1681 after he saw the small class of 1677 graduate. For the college as a whole, however, such wild fluctuations must have brought real problems of both day-to-day logistics and forward planning.

Edinburgh's library, as has been seen, began with the 268 theological works, valued at 1,000 merks, left in 1580 by Clement Little in his will. The growth of the library is a subject which is difficult to quantify with much precision before 1636, when a catalogue of its holdings is extant, but there can be little doubt that the Little bequest formed the major part of the collections for some considerable time. There can be little doubt that, in its early years, it came nowhere near to rivalling the library of Trinity College, Dublin, founded some years after Edinburgh's college, which had almost 4,000 books detailed in its catalogue drawn up in 1610, still less the 7,500 works recorded in 1615 in the collection at Oxford assembled by Sir Thomas Bodley. Individual, minor bequests, sometimes of single books may have trickled in, especially from students on graduation: fifty individual donations of this kind were recorded in 1634. Yet the sixty-one books donated in the same year by Mr Willam Struthers, one of the burgh's ministers, was exceptional for its size. At some point the practice began of devoting the fees paid to laureate on book purchases; 139 books were bought on these proceeds in 1635. What is certain, however, is that the library was accommodated in the same small room from 1583 until 1626. Yet the library catalogue of 1636 lists some 3,018 volumes and an accommodation crisis cannot have been far off. Until 1635 it was a library without a librarian, until 1636 one without regulations and, until 1646, one without dedicated premises, with its books exposed in the upper part of the public hall of the college to the threat of leaky windows and damp air. A new building was finally completed in 1644, it being the result of an outside benefaction.

From about that point onwards, if not before, the library's holdings may have begun to accumulate more rapidly. Lists of books donated by graduates are recorded, though intermittently, from 1634 onwards, there is a record of money being diverted from matriculation fees towards book purchasing from

1653 onwards: £70 was devoted to this in that year, but although the accounts continue there is no further trace of using them to subside the library again until 1667. There is no general record of library purchasing that survives before 1693. By then, it is clear that systematic efforts were being made to improve provision: £325 was spent on books bought in London and a further £206 for volumes acquired in 'Holland' in 1694.

Bequests to the college were not conspicuous early on in its history. On the contrary, the habitual resort of the town council was either to force taxation (on which there was a natural ceiling, especially in the early decades of the seventeenth century when taxation became virtually annual) or heavy-handed appeals to the 'benevolence of the nichtbouris'. It took time for the college to gain the affection of would-be benefactors. According to a book of mortifications drawn up by the council in 1656, thirty-nine bequests, all but two of them from private individuals and totalling £71,000, were received between 1597 and 1655. Only two of these private bequests, however, amounted to more than £1,000 in the period up to 1638 and one of those was from a nobleman; the average was for £200 or £300. In assessing such sums, it needs to be remembered that the Scots pound was worth only one-twelfth of sterling for virtually all of this period. By far the most popular beneficiary was the divinity school, and especially the salary and maintenance of the Professor of Divinity, which suggests that this particular largesse may have been due to a certain amount of prompting from the pulpits of the burgh. Only a handful of bequests were specified for bursaries to students before the 1640s. And a mere couple of modest bequests were for the purchase of books. One bequest, which oddly was not recorded in this inventory, was the unspecified gift of 7,000 merks made by a local merchant in 1646; it was vired towards the building of a new library. On the other hand, another gift of 1646 made to the libraries of all the Scottish universities and colleges somehow ended up as bursaries for Edinburgh divinity students.

Institutional support was rare and tended to come with strings attached. The first significant bequest was a sum of £3,000 from the law lords and the upper reaches of Edinburgh's legal fraternity in 1597. Although notionally devoted to the support of a master of humanity and six bursars, it was not unconnected with the desire to set up legal teaching within the college. In 1608, a bequest of £8,100, from the Edinburgh general kirk session, carried not one but two price tags: it took the form of a capital sum on which the council paid a generous rate of 8.5 per cent interest to top up the salaries of the masters; and it demanded a greater role for the burgh's ministers in appointments. The first large-scale bequest was made in 1640, and again it was devoted to the chair of divinity: the sum of 26,000 merks was left by Bartilmo Somerville of Saughtonhall, who seems profitably to have combined piety and usury. He was one of Edinburgh's most successful money-lenders, who had made good and bought a local landed estate. Most of the residue of what he left in his will, some 10,000 merks, was left to the 'good cause of the Covenant'. Although the total capital was valued by the town treasurer in 1656 as worth £71,000, a number of mortifications were made on the regular income from property; such investments suffered badly from the collapse of credit, falling rents and the downturn in the burgh economy that accompanied the latter years of the Wars of the Covenant and the Cromwellian occupation that followed.

These are not unexpected conclusions, but one last contrast between England's and Scotland's universities in the early seventeenth century is more surprising. About 35 per cent of English graduates entered the church. In Scotland, in what Professor Hugh Trevor-Roper once notoriously called a theocratic and clergy-ridden society, the figure was far less – at both Edinburgh and elsewhere – standing at about 20 per cent in the 1620s. The wider implications of this sharp contrast cannot be explored here but they do give some reason for doubting the familiar description of Edinburgh's college in the seventeenth century as its 'Genevan phase'. The Scottish figure for entrants to the ministry may be artificially depressed because it is not possible to count those who took a first step to the ministry via a post as dominie in a parish school. On the other hand, there was undoubtedly a widespread scramble for jobs in seventeenth-century Scotland among the sons of the various classes which made up the new 'middling sort', ranging from the new landed feuars and heritors, who had acquired land and status for the first time in the aftermath of the feuing of church lands, to the swelling ranks of the *bourgeoisie*. All of them had ambitions for their sons beyond the old resort of craft or trade. There for all to see, and especially in Edinburgh, were the opportunities of a new economy, with a substantially expanded service sector and a surfeit of capital to invest.

The most awkward of many difficulties in writing about the 'tounis college' in the first century of its existence is knowing what to call it. Sir Archibald Grant in his two-volume history of the university, written in 1884 to mark its tercentenary, was insistent that it should not be called a university – as had been done in previous histories – for it did not itself use that term before 1685. There is some justice in this view, without needing to call up the legal doubts raised and settled in the nineteenth century about its status and right to confer degrees. On the other hand, the story of Edinburgh in the seventeenth century had much in common with other *arriviste* institutions of higher learning throughout much of continental Europe. The new institutions steadily appropriated to themselves the trappings of university status: beadles, maces, the distinctive if outlandish academic dress, elaborate laureation ceremonies, commemorations of benefactors and the like. Edinburgh appointed a rector in 1620, acquired a mace by 1640 (which was used to process the Rector on ceremonial occasions), began to call regents 'professors' from the 1620s onwards (though the incumbents continued with the same hard slog of regenting with occasional public lectures now added to their workload), started to refer to the 'Faculty' or the 'whole Faculty' from 1668 on, conferred its first honorary degree in 1695 (ironically in civil law, a subject which it did not teach), and by the end of the century was referring to the 'Senatus Academicus'. Even its students had a good conceit of themselves: an 'advertisement' of 1680, justifying the burning of an effigy of the pope as Anti-Christ, referred to them as the 'students of the Royal University of Edinburgh'. Academic ceremony fitted well enough into the existing civic ceremony of what was still a capital city, accustomed to seeing the formal rituals of the riding of parliament, processions of the law lords and inaugurations of lord provosts.

From another point of view, Edinburgh was, by the Restoration period, probably caught in a tension between two sets of ambitions for its college. Should it try to outdo its pre-Reformation university rivals by imitating them even further? Or should it try to carve out for itself a distinctive niche that set it and its curriculum apart from Glasgow and St Andrews especially? This was a dilemma faced by institutions elsewhere. In 1636 the distinguished Calvinist theologian Gisbertus Voetius (1589–1676) delivered his inaugural lecture at the new, chartered University of Utrecht. He took as his theme the difference between universities, devoted to the *studium generale* and able to recruit on a national basis, and what he called 'illustrious schools', which often reflected the strongly felt desire on the part of urban authorities to extend civic culture to its citizens as well as to educate its youth. This distinction was the basis of a long-standing quarrel between the University of Leiden, anxious to preserve its monopoly in conferring degrees, and a planned 'illustrious school' in nearby Amsterdam, a fast-expanding metropolis, which saw its project as a civic enterprise. To translate this into the context of Edinburgh (which Voetius considered as an 'illustrious school'), there were, the more the seventeenth century progressed, two sets of tensions.

The first lay between its role as a civic-run college, answerable to the town council as its patron, mentor and funder, and its instincts to run itself as a self-enclosed *academia*. What kind of graduates did the college want to produce? Was it there to produce better-qualified candidates for the new civic and consumer society or was it still a quasi-clerical seminary? The number who dropped out, after a preliminary year or so, suggests that society was coming to recognise that the level of education suitable for *fonctionnaires* of the state, law or commerce – as distinct from the church – did not necessarily entail a full-blown four-year degree. The second dilemma concerned the question of whether the college should have a wider role in the construction of a new kind of civic society, and how it should relate to the other institutions jostling for position and recognition in the capital. These included the Faculty of Advocates (a body which as early as 1582 had a 'dene' as its head), the College of Physicians (which finally acquired 'royal', chartered status in 1681) and the College of Surgeons (which by 1694 had shed its barber surgeon roots and acquired monopoly status in anatomy). Their very names – of 'faculty' and 'college' – are suggestive of the institutional rivalries which were rife in seventeenth-century Edinburgh. Each could claim, more so than the college, to be making a dynamic contribution to a metropolitan culture. As for the town college itself, it retrospectively claimed, in 1685, that it had been 'erected in ane University and indewed with the privalledge of erecting professions of all sorts particullarly of medicin'. In other words, it here seemed to aspire to become another University of Leiden, which saw itself as a professional institution producing lawyers, physicians and specialist divines.

It is in one or other of these two contexts that the much-heralded developments which took place in the curriculum and in appointments in the 1670s and 1680s should be viewed. Prominent among the developments were a familiarity with the ideas of Isaac Newton, especially on light and colour, and the acquiring of his *Principia* (1687) for the Library soon after its publication. There seems to have been a growing, general interest in experimental science, which can be traced from the 1680s onwards, mostly via the content of students' lecture notes, some of which seem to have been peddled from one generation of students to the next, and graduation theses. By the late 1670s and the 1680s, too, Cartesian physics had

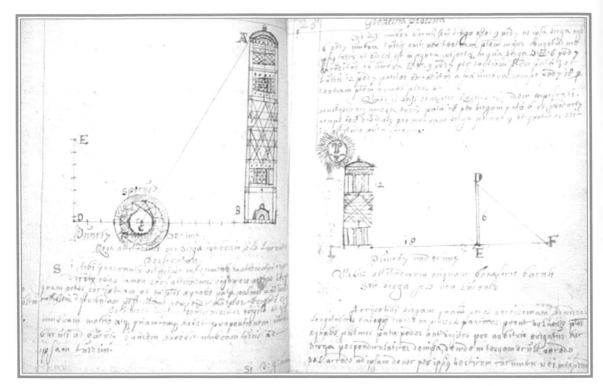

appeared, though often still figuring alongside Aristotelian, even in the same lectures. Although most of these developments were common to all the Scottish universities, it was in Edinburgh, so it has been claimed, that the largest concentration of regents expounding Newtonian philosophy was to be found. This, allied to the successive appointments as Professor of Mathematics of James Gregory in 1674 and his nephew David in 1683, makes a strong case for a curriculum which was showing distinct signs of being progressive and responsive to new ideas. The relative slowness and piecemeal way with which these ideas came to the surface, however, is to be explained by the dynamics through which they were disseminated.

The duties of the two Gregories were hardly onerous: they seem to have consisted of two public lectures a week, given to all students, who attended with their regents. One can imagine that tutors as well as pupils struggled to absorb the new ideas – with varying degrees of success among both constituencies. Without more systematic or extensive exposure within the curriculum, it is hardly surprising that Newtonian and other

The student notes of Francis Pringle, future Professor of Greek at St Andrews, on the lectures of David Gregory, 'Geometria Praxtica', which covered optics, dynamics and mechanics as well as mathematics. Illustrated here are notes on the measurement of the height of distant objects. (Edinburgh University Library, Special Collections)

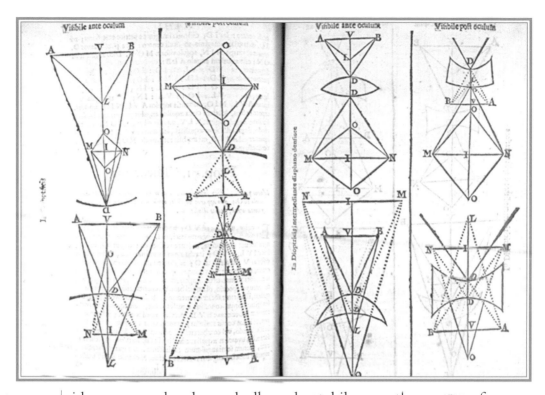

Visibile ante oculum   Visibile post oculum   Visibile ante oculum   Visibile post oculum

ideas appeared only gradually and patchily over the course of the last quarter of the century and beyond. The same applied, though probably with more force, to medical teaching. The appointment of three professors of medicine in 1685 hardly marked a milestone. None had a salary or any teaching duties. But it was part of the effort of town council and college to stake out territory for themselves, as a 'University' with 'privalledge', in opposition to the new College of Physicians. Whether the appointment of what were little more than what might now be termed research professors or visiting professorial fellows had any real impact is questionable. It is likely that these glamorous appointments made headlines but not much more. What certainly remained was the division, now accentuated, between the college hierarchy and the ordinary workforce of regents, sometimes also confusingly given the title of 'professor' but not the pay or conditions of the new-style professoriat. James Gregory's salary is unknown but is unlikely to have been less than the £1,000 a year paid to his nephew, who doubled the stipend which he earned at St Andrews when he moved to Edinburgh. This was a sum matched only by (well-endowed) professors of divinity (such as Lawrence Charteris, appointed on 1,600 merks a year in 1675) or by the Principal, who often (as in the case of Andrew Cant, appointed in the same year) combined the two posts; Cant was paid 2,000 merks. Lesser 'professors' were paid only a fraction of these sums. James Gregory's colleague, George Sinclair, although also titled 'professor of mathematics', earned less than £200 per annum.

Whether the lectures of the new breed of 'super-professors' had a regular, wider audience is unknown. James Gregory gave his inaugural lecture in 1674 to an audience which included the town council as patrons and a cross-section of the Edinburgh establishment. The fact that it was in Latin would have been no barrier. So too was the inaugural oration given by Sir George Mackenzie of Rosehaugh on the occasion of the opening of the Advocates' Library in 1689. Beyond that, it is possible only to guess. It is here that the silence of the records, of both burgh and college, is at its most frustrating. The wider impact of the college on the intellectual atmosphere of Edinburgh in the Restoration period cannot be gauged with any precision. It seems unlikely, however, that the civic and aristocratic values which imbued the new Edinburgh, as it was intended to be, were divorced from the role cast for the college by its patrons. One clue towards this is provided by the arrangements for laureation, which became an elaborate rite of passage for the new entrants into civil society, conducted before an audience which consisted of members of the privy council and aristocracy as well as the Edinburgh establishment.

The 1670s and 1680s were, as it might now be put, times of opportunity as well as challenge for institutions of higher learning. The core mission of the university was, as a set of regulations of 1668 for the conduct of the *disputatio* insisted, the inculcation of 'faith and good manners'. Although this has a later 'enlightened' whiff about it, these two objectives had been present from the earliest days of the town college. The preservation of 'faith' required the identification and refutation of error, which meant that the old methods of dividing, sub-dividing and contradicting philosophical propositions were still used. They were, indeed, all the more difficult and necessary in an age when error, in the view of the establishment, was spreading at an alarming rate, peddled by intellectual enemies ranging from Jesuits to conventiclers. This familiar battle was given an extra bite in the Restoration period, with an increasingly agitated state church trying to enforce religious uniformity in the face of opposition, which ranged from moderate dissent within Edinburgh itself to sedition and outright rebellion of radical Covenanters in parts of the south-west. The 1668 statutes seem to have been particularly exercised by heresies which cast doubt on the doctrine of the Trinity, but increasingly the battlefield was populated by Covenanting propagandists. The list of books officially banned by the state soared: eight were proscribed in the 1660s, three in the 1670s and twenty-one during the 1680s. As always, the universities were seen as potential breeding grounds for dissident ideas and they, too, would be subjected to increasing scrutiny by the authorities of town and state.

The appointments to glamorous new chairs were part of a wider campaign waged by two successive principals – Andrew Cant (1675–85) and Alexander Monro (1685–90), both former professors of divinity at St Andrews – to claim for the town college a new role in both Edinburgh and national life. Inevitably, part of the price to be paid for being based in the capital city was political and religious conformity. By the 1680s, it had become customary for the Lord Provost to be nominated by the privy council. By the reign of James VII and II (1685–9), who had spent over two years in the capital between 1679 and 1681, it became usual for the annual elections to be held off until the royal pleasure was known. Increasing interference from the crown also had tangible benefits, for both the capital and its college. In 1688, both royal burgh and what was now restored as 'King James' University' received a new charter. For the town council, by this time virtually a branch office of the privy council, there were real advantages in this new level of royal patronage. The elaborate and sweeping confirmation of the rights of 'a full and ample University' had a double benefit. It was given the right to grant degrees in a long list of subjects which included law and medicine as well as philosophy, languages and theology, which helped fend off the claims of the rival institutions in the capital. Furthermore, the conferring on the Lord Provost, Magnus Prince and his successors, of the office of Chancellor of the University kept at bay the ambitions of the Bishop of Edinburgh to gain control of the college. This was no idle threat; two years earlier, Bishop Paterson had been granted the title of Chancellor 'of the College or University' although parliament had refused to ratify the appointment. In turn, the Principal of the University was made Vice-Chancellor. The rights of patronage of town over gown were clarified and strengthened, but so too were the powers of the crown over the capital.

With both Lord Provost and Principal firmly attached to the royal court, new levels of outside interference were in process of being imposed on the fledgling 'university' when the revolution crisis hit Edinburgh in 1688. A royal visitation of the universities had been set in motion in 1687, and changes had been made in the same year to the oath required of graduates; the dropping of the word 'reformed' from the promise to adhere to the 'Christian religion' seemed particularly portentous.

Opinion in both Edinburgh and its university is harder to gauge than certain events of 1688–9 might indicate. The fact that students joined the Edinburgh mob which ransacked the Thistle Chapel at Holyrood, which had been fitted out for Catholic worship, should not be taken as conclusive evidence of the balance of opinion within either the university or the Edinburgh establishment. Ironically, the revolution 'settlement', with James VII deposed by parliament three months later and the crown conferred on William and Mary, brought more rather than less outside interference in the affairs of the university. Following an act passed by parliament in July 1690, a full-scale visitation of the universities was instituted. It became a witch-hunt, part of the purging of both the parish ministry and academia not only of Episcopalian sympathisers but also a large section of moderate Presbyterian opinion. Nationally, it was a purge on a greater scale than any that went before it, including those at the Reformation of 1560 and the Restoration of 1660.

In Edinburgh, prominent Episcopalian or royalist sympathisers generally escaped; they included Sibbald and Mackenzie of Rosehaugh, the moving forces behind the College of Physicians and the Advocates' Library respectively. The university did not escape so lightly. The visitation committee that examined Edinburgh University had Alexander Monro as its prime target but four other masters were also dismissed, including Dr John Strachan, Professor of Divinity. Monro's replacement as Principal, appointed a day after his dismissal in September 1690, was Dr Gilbert Rule, one of his inquisitors. The story of the first century of the town's college ends as it began. A purge brought it into being in the form it took in October 1583 – a liberal arts college rather than a Presbyterian seminary. Another purge, in 1690, formed the prelude for a further attempt to transform its role – this time from 'King James's University' into a strict Presbyterian college.

PART II

The Making of an Enlightened University

Nicholas Phillipson

Museum, Hall, Library

The Glorious Revolution and the Revolution Settlement are famous in England for providing a bloodless
and moderate solution to the constitutional turmoil of
the previous half-century. Things were rather different in
Scotland. The parliament that offered William of Orange and
his wife the throne was dominated by a radical, Presbyterian
nobility and gentry set on restoring the Presbyterian church
and limiting the powers of the crown over parliament. It led to
a settlement which was distrusted by the new king, by Jacobites
and by Episcopalians and it sparked off a Jacobite rebellion in
1689, which was put down by force at Killiecrankie. All of this
had important consequences for the Scottish universities and
particularly for Edinburgh. In 1690 a parliamentary visitation
was set up to purge the schools and universities of those who
refused to take the oath of allegiance to the king and to
subscribe to the Confession of Faith of the newly restored
Presbyterian kirk, a purge which, in the case of Edinburgh, led
to the 'extrusion' of Principal Munro and the Professor of
Divinity, John Strachan. This was followed by the appointment
of a distinguished strict Presbyterian, Gilbert Rule as Munro's
successor, and the beginning of a period of reform which
proved abortive but was to have a lasting though unexpected
influence on the university's development.

By 1690 Rule was probably in his early sixties. He had
grown up in the heady days of the civil war and interregnum,
when it seemed for a few years as though Scotland would be
turned into a radical, Presbyterian polity. The universities were
to play an important part in this process of renewal as an
educational machine which would supply the country with a
godly clergy and a godly laity. University curricula were to be
reformed and standardised. A new, doctrinally pure textbook of
philosophy was to be devised and circulated throughout the
universities to keep the whole system together. After all, as John
Knox had warned the General Assembly in 1572: 'Above all
things, preserve the Church from the bondage of the
Universities. Persuade them to rule themselves peaceably, and
order their schools in Christ; but subject never the pulpit to

their judgement, neither yet exempt them from your jurisdiction.' Nothing happened but the Covenanting plan had a profound influence on the young Gilbert Rule. He had been appointed regent at Glasgow in 1651 and had fallen under the influence of its charismatic Principal, Robert Baillie, the architect of these projected university reforms. After the Restoration he had been 'outed' for refusing to use the new book of common prayer and had gone into exile to Leiden, where he had studied medicine. He had returned to Scotland in 1680 in the mistaken belief that the Earl of Haddington would be able to protect him. But the Episcopalian privy council was determined to be rid of an influential Presbyterian nuisance and Rule was imprisoned on the Bass Rock on a trumped-up charge and only released on condition that he got out of Scotland. After a second exile in Dublin earning a living as a dissenting minister and physician, he returned to Scotland in 1688, an elderly, eminent and grimly determined martyr to the Presbyterian cause, determined to do what he could to steer the newly restored kirk and the universities in an orthodox Presbyterian direction.

At first, the town council looked on the revolution as an opportunity to develop the college's potential as an 'illustrious school' by petitioning the crown for funds to establish chairs of law and medicine, to restock the library, to purchase mathematical instruments and to repair the college steeple. However, the new privy council was more interested in turning the college into a seminary for training up a new generation of Presbyterian clergy. The sum of £300 per annum was given to each of the universities to establish new chairs of divinity and bursaries for divinity students. Rule saw this as a welcome first step in the great project of regenerating the Scottish university system on orthodox principles. He had been *praeses* of the committee set up by the visitors to apply the tests to the Edinburgh faculty in 1690 and to 'extrude' those who refused to swear the oath of allegiance and to subscribe to the Confession of Faith. In 1692 he was put on another privy council committee to inquire into the teaching and 'the general good' of the Scottish universities, and to tighten up the traditional, scholastic system of teaching philosophy that had been falling into disrepair during the Restoration, an initiative that the Aberdeen Colleges and St Andrews obstructed to the best of their ability. In 1695 he joined a third, even more ambitious privy council committee for producing the doctrinally pure philosophy textbook on which the new curriculum of the Scottish universities was to be based. The enterprise was a disaster. Once again the universities only co-operated reluctantly and squabbled endlessly over drafts of different sections of the text. No one's heart was in the experiment except Rule's, and when he died in 1701 his favourite scheme died with him, unloved and unlamented.

Rule was no more successful in turning the Tounis College into an orthodox Presbyterian college than he was in radicalising the university system generally. Not satisfied with 'extruding' the former Principal and Professor of Divinity for refusing to take the oaths and subscribe to the Confession of Faith, he decided to dig deeper into the beliefs of the members of faculty who had subscribed the oaths. Their lecture notes and those of their students were minutely scrutinised for signs of doctrinal and moral impurity. They themselves were subjected to lengthy examinations. It was what indignant Episcopalians called a 'Presbyterian inquisition' which resulted in the extrusion of the Professor of Hebrew and two regents and the departure of the Professor of Mathematics, David Gregory, for Oxford and their replacement by men of unimpeachable mediocrity. The suspicion that Presbyterian orthodoxy was narrow, intolerant and divisive was reinforced in 1696–7 by the trial and execution of a former student, Thomas Aikenhead, for blasphemously denying the divinity of Christ.

But the problem of providing the college with a doctrinally correct faculty was as nothing compared with the problem of dealing with student unrest. From the 1680s to the early eighteenth century, student unrest in Edinburgh was endemic. The reasons for this are not clear, though they must have had something to do with the fact that the college had no residential accommodation and that students in their late teens were free to live where and how they liked in a period of profound political and religious turmoil. This unrest continued unabated throughout Rule's reign. In 1701 the town council attempted to impose a code of conduct which forbade playing games, throwing stones, even walking on the streets. Taverns and ale

ACT

Against Tumults and Disorders in Colledges and Universities.

At *Edinburgh*, the Twenty sixth day of *December* 1693 years.

THE LORDS of Their Majesties Privy Council, ordains the Act of Privy Council of the Date the ninth day of *March* last, against Tumults & other Disorders of Students in Colledges, whereof the Tenor follows: AT *EDINBURGH*, the ninth day of *March*, One thousand six hundred and ninety three years, The Lords of Their Majesties Privy Council taking to their consideration the Tumults and Disorders which frequently fall out amongst, & are committed by the Students within the several Colledges and Universities within this Kingdom; and having considered the Report of a Committee of their own number, appointed in this matter, THE SAIDS LORDS for preventing of any Tumults or other Disorders in any of the saids Colledges and Universities for the future, Do hereby Authorize and Impower the several Principals, Regents and Masters of the saids Colledges *respective*, in case it shall happen hereafter any of the Students of any of the Colledges above-mentioned, to commit, or be guilty of any Tumults, or other enormous Disorders, against the quiet and good Government of the saids Colledgs; to impose and exact Fines from such as they shall find guilty, not exceeding the respective Rates and Proportions after-mentioned, *viz.* For a Nobleman, or his eldest Son, an hundred and fifty Pounds *Scots*, for Noblemens younger Sons, or Barons, themselves, or their eldest Sons, an hundred Pounds, for the younger Sons of Barons or Gentlemen, and for the Sons of Burgesses fifty Pounds; and for the Sons of Crafts-men or Yeamen fifty Merks *Scots*, and that by and attour the Reparation of Damnages: And the saids Lords do hereby Require and Command the Magistrats of the respective Burghs where the saids Colledges are kept, to interpose their Authority to the Sentence of the saids Masters, and to give them their assistance in executing the same, by Imprisonment, if need beis; and allows and appoints the Sums that shall be exacted for Fines, in manner, and for the causes above-mentioned, to be applyed for the use of the several Bibliothicks of the saids Colledges. And the saids Lords having reviewed an Act of Council, of the date the first day of *February*, One thousand six hundred and seventy two years, prohibiting one Colledge to receive any Schollar from another Colledge: They do restrict the same to such Schollars only as have been removed for Misdemeanors, or have fled from Discipline, TO BE PRINTED and Published at the Mercat-Crosses of *Edinburgh*, New and Old *Aberdenes*, Saint *Andrews* and *Glasgow*, and likewise to be publickly Read before the Students, in the Common-Schools, or Publick-Halls of all the Universities and Colledges within this Kingdom, and Printed Copies thereof to be affixed upon the Doors of the saids Universities and Colledges. Extracted by me

Per Actum Dominorum Secreti Concilii
GILB. ELIOT, *Cls. Sti Concilii.*

GOD save King VVilliam and Queen Mary.

Edinburgh, Printed by the Successors of *Andrew Anderson*, Printers to Their Most Excellent Majesties, *Anno DOM.* 1694.

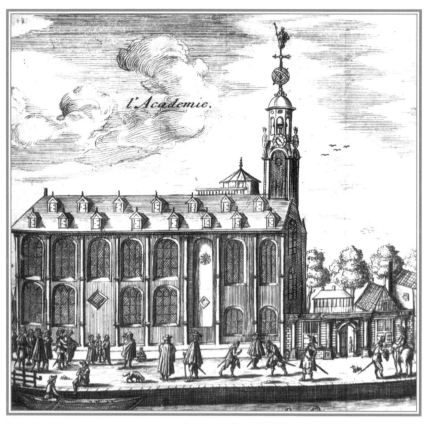

l'Academie.

houses were placed out of bounds. The carrying of weapons was forbidden. Blasphemy, profanity or 'talking smutty or obscene' was to be punished by fines, which students generally refused to pay. Three years later things were just as bad and the town council was still complaining of the decay of good order and decency 'whereby severall disorders are committed which does exceedingly reflect upon the government of the Colledge'.

Rule died in 1701, his grand design for the Scottish universities in tatters, his governance of the Tounis College a disaster. Indeed his only positive contribution to the great goal of preserving Presbyterian orthodoxy had been to remove suspect books from the library to the safety of his own rooms. The college was in an impossible position. It was neither an 'illustrious school' or a productive Presbyterian seminary. It had nothing to offer a government in search of a moderate clergy, or gentlemen in search of a polite professional education for their sons. To make matters worse, the rapidly dwindling number of students was depriving the regents and professors of their livelihood. As the Faculty put it in a piteous petition to the Scottish parliament in 1707,

> The Sellaries of the far greater part of your Grace and Lo[rdships] petitioners are less by halfe than those of any other of the Professors in the rest of the Universities of this Kingdome, and the number of their Students are of late much decreased by the encouradgement that Gentlemen have to breed their sons in the Army, and the small advantage they can propose by following Letters at home when all professions are so numerous that the one halfe can hardly make bread.

Perhaps the most striking aspect of Rule's administration was his total lack of interest in the city's lively local educational market. During the 1690s Edinburgh's social life was dominated by the nobility, gentry and professional classes, people with sons to educate and the money to pay for it. During the Restoration, those who could afford to do so sent their sons to the great Dutch universities at Leiden and Utrecht for a professional and gentlemanly education. For wealthy students, like the young John Clerk of Penicuik, these visits could last three or four years and could involve studying 'polite' subjects such as French, Italian, Music and the Fine Arts; in Clerk's case this was followed by a grand tour of France and Italy. For others, a Dutch education meant a shorter, cheaper period of study, lasting a few months or even a few weeks, but long enough to allow the student to catch a glimpse of a cosmopolitan Calvinist system of education of unrivalled sophistication that was very different to their own. Indeed, so popular was Dutch education between the 1660s and the 1720s that it had become part of the normal education of the better-off landed and professional classes of central Scotland.

But Dutch education was expensive – a two-year course in civil law or medicine cost more than £100 per annum. To cater for those who could not afford the real thing, the town council began licensing private teachers to teach subjects such as anatomy, botany, chemistry, Scots law and civil law. Most of these teachers made their money by training surgeons' apprentices and law clerks. The more ambitious had their eyes on the lucrative gentlemanly market and began offering classes in subjects such as French, Italian, fencing and dancing. It is interesting that some of these teachers were allowed to call themselves 'professor' and some were even allowed to teach in the college classrooms. By the early eighteenth century one or two of these private teachers had gone so far as to set up little academies of their own, teaching subjects which were not on offer in Rule's college. In 1704 John Spottiswoode offered classes in law, mathematics, grammar, logic and rhetoric, history and philology in the hope, as his prospectus put it, that 'this would cultivate in your minds and actions religion and vertue'. A year later William Cockburn established 'a college or lecture on Moral and Political Learning' which would provide 'a solid foundation for Law or Divinity and endue Gentlemen with many Conspicuous Qualifications suitable to their Characters'.

There was an educational opportunity here which could not be ignored indefinitely, and it was not surprising that after Rule's death the town council should have decided to introduce the teaching of law and medicine into the curriculum. What was much more surprising was the scale of these reforms. Between 1703 and 1726, the entire curriculum and method of teaching it was remodelled on the Leiden model. It was an experiment that took time to complete and had somewhat mixed results. But it laid the foundations of a system of college education that made it possible for Edinburgh to develop as the most admired enlightened university in the west.

The main architect of these reforms was William Carstares, Principal from 1703 to 1715. Like Rule, William Carstares was a well-known Presbyterian statesman who had suffered for his faith and had gone into exile in Holland during the Restoration. But he was a Presbyterian of a very different sort;

one orthodox minister, Robert Wodrow denounced him and his friends as 'modern Presbyterians ... of the court [who] have got new light'. Carstares' Presbyterianism was more inclusive, less suspicious of civil society than Rule's. He was also a political heavyweight who had been chaplain and advisor to William of Orange, the future William III. He was a long-standing admirer of Leiden University and was never in any doubt that it was the right model for Edinburgh – he even hoped to attract Dutch professors. Like the king, Carstares wanted a university that would train up a moderately minded clergy, which was inclusive in its attitude to religious differences, and was, above all, ready to shake off the kirk's radical past. Like the town council he wanted a university which would attract the better-off and students from England and abroad. By the time of his death in 1715 new chairs of public law, civil law, anatomy and chemistry had been established. The dormant chair of ecclesiastical history was revived. William Hamilton, a moderate Presbyterian and a seminal influence on the development of Presbyterian thinking, was appointed Professor of Divinity in 1709. Carstares also used his political influence to secure the substantial sum of £300 per annum from the crown for general purposes. His only major setback was his failure to find the money to open a boarding house for English dissenting students.

But the cornerstone of Carstares' reforms was a radical reorganisation of the system of teaching. The teaching of Greek, which had previously been shared between the regents, was now assigned to a single professor. The regenting system itself – which worked on the principle that each cohort of students would be taken through the four parts of the philosophy course by a single regent – was abolished in favour of a professorial system that assigned each of the divisions of the curriculum to a single professor. As at Leiden, professors were now expected to deliver public 'colleges' on their subjects and were allowed to offer private 'colleges' on related subjects to those that wanted them. Whereas Rule's college had been 'a Presbyterian seminary with a philosophy school attached', Carstares'

college offered a two-year core course in the classics followed by a two-year course in philosophy to be taken as a prelude to professional study of divinity, law or medicine. The Dutch influence on these reforms was profound. The town council justified the new system on the grounds that 'all the parts of philosophy would be taught in two years, as they are in the most famous universities abroad [i.e. in Holland]'. It defended the new chair of civil law on the ground that it would spare parents the expense of sending their sons abroad, and the new chair of chemistry on the grounds that it was 'through the want of professors of physick and chymistry in this kingdome the youth who have applyed themselves to study have been necessitated to travel abroad a considerable time for their education to the great prejudice of the nation by the necessary charges occasioned thereby'. It was the first stage of an attempt to lure wealthier Scots back to Edinburgh with the sort of education they had hitherto only been able to get abroad.

Glasgow College, 1693, from Slezer's *Theatrum Scotiae*. Francis Hutcheson's experiments in the teaching of moral philosophy at Glasgow were regarded with envy in Edinburgh by the town council and by moderate Presbyterian students. (Edinburgh University Library, Special Collections)

Carstares died in 1715 before his reforms could be developed and it took another fifteen years to complete them. The fact that the town council, the new Provost, George Drummond, and the new Principal, William Wishart, were prepared to carry them through says something about their determination but more about the political realities of post-Union Scotland. This was the period which saw the consolidation of Whig power in London under Sir Robert Walpole and the rise to power in Scotland of one of Walpole's closest friends, the Earl of Ilay, later 3rd Duke of Argyll.

By the mid-1720s Ilay had become Scottish 'manager' and would remain so for much of the time before his death in 1761. His access to the vast government patronage machine allowed him to establish effective control over the Scottish electoral system, over government and over the General Assembly. When he visited Edinburgh he held court at Holyrood, waited on by the judges, magistrates and professors in their gowns. In fact, as contemporaries often commented, he had become the 'uncrowned King of Scotland'. His influence over the town council and the college was to be decisive – Lord Provost Drummond was one of his political agents. But Ilay was an interesting oddity, something of a scholar as well as a great machine politician. He had studied chemistry at Leiden with the great Herman Boerhaave and had his own laboratory. He took a keen interest in mathematics and was a Fellow of the Royal Society. He understood the importance of universities in shaping the religious and political culture of a modern state. He was as responsible as Wishart and the town council for completing the reform process Carstares had begun and in making sure that most university chairs were filled with good scholars rather than placemen – provided, of course, that they were politically acceptable.

These reforms took place in a city that was changing in important ways. At the time of the Union, it had been feared that Edinburgh would lose its aristocratic society as well as its parliament and privy council, and, for a time, it looked as though this might happen. The great nobility abandoned their town houses in the Canongate and took the high road to London; the minor nobility and gentry retired to their estates. By the 1720s, however, change was in the air. London was expensive and remote and the minor nobility and gentry were beginning to return to the city for the winter months to do their political and legal business and to enjoy themselves. Their sons were were now being sent to the College rather than Leiden. The Faculty of Advocates and the College of Physicians and the Surgeons' Incorporation seemed interested in developing professional education in the city. Carstares' Dutch strategy was beginning to pay off and the town council was anxious to develop it. A chair of Scots law was founded in 1722, under the joint patronage of the town council and the Faculty of Advocates. A chair of universal history was created in 1719 to provide 'such professions in our colleges, as enable our youth to study with equal advantages at home as they do abroad'. The spectacularly opportunistic appointment of Sir Isaac Newton's star pupil, Colin McLaurin, to the chair of mathematics in 1725 was justified on the grounds 'that it was impossible for us to hope for any opportunity of doing a thing more honourable and advantageous for the city, that could contribute more to the reputation of the university, and advance the interest of learning in this country, than the giving Mr McLaurin suitable encouragement to settle among us'.

By far the most ambitious and important part of this Dutch strategy was the founding of the medical faculty in 1726. The founding of chairs of anatomy and chemistry in 1705 and 1711 had introduced medical teaching into the university but had left the control of medical education and the licensing of practitioners to the College of Physicians and the College of Surgeons. It is hard not to believe that the possibility of creating a degree-giving faculty of medicine in the college was not discussed at the time. Not only was there an obvious demand for university medical education from the better-off, it was clear that there was a lively demand for practical medical education from the surgeon-apprentices who received their professional training from the Surgeons' Incorporation. What is

Sir George
Drummond, by Sir
George Chalmers.
He was Lord Provost
of Edinburgh and
the Duke of Argyll's
principal ally and
agent in the city.
(Scottish National
Portrait Gallery)

more, Carstares had been a close friend of the Edinburgh surgeon John Monro, another Presbyterian, who had gone into exile on account of his faith during the Restoration, had studied medicine at Leiden and had returned to Edinburgh, anxious to see medicine taught in the college on the Leiden model. He set up as a surgeon-apothecary and became Dean of the Surgeon's Incorporation in 1712–13, an appointment that gave him a seat on the town council and a say in college affairs. Lord Provost Drummond and Ilay were both interested. Monro, being a man who liked working through others, and had his family's interests at heart, sent his son Alexander to Leiden to study medicine and, on his return, got him appointed Professor of Anatomy in 1719.

Alexander lost no time in developing a new system of medical education to train surgeon-apprentices, for membership of the Surgeons' Incorporation. He invited the King's

Botanist, Charles Alston, and the Professor of Chemistry, James Crawford, to contribute to the course and, between them, they constructed a surprisingly comprehensive curriculum, which involved the study of anatomy, chemistry, medical theory and medical practice. But the Surgeons' Incorporation was not allowed to award degrees and its course lacked the academic glamour enjoyed by the academic course at Leiden. Monro's achievement was to persuade the town council, the College of Physicians and the College of Surgeons to transfer the business of medical education to the university, telling them that he would make Edinburgh 'as famous a school of Anatomy as any of those to which our youth is sent with so great expense for their education' and that he would be 'the principal instrument of setting on foot a complete system of medicine in this place'. Four new professors of medicine – with no salaries, but with the power to charge fees – were appointed by the town council and given the power 'to examine candidates, and to do every-thing requisite and necessary to the graduation of Doctor of Medicine'.

The Tounis College continued to develop as a 'Dutch'

college between 1726 and 1745. The inspiration behind its new curriculum and most of the new chairs was Dutch and many of the professors teaching at the time of the Forty-Five had studied in Holland, including all of the medical professors. What is more, as a prospectus of 1741 shows, most of the textbooks used in the teaching of divinity, law and medicine and many of those used in the teaching of philosophy were the same as those used in Leiden and Utrecht. But it was one thing to plant a Dutch system in Edinburgh, another to see how the plant would develop. There can be no doubt that the general level of teaching throughout the college was conscientious, and good enough to encourage parents to send their sons to Edinburgh rather than Leiden or Utrecht. Nevertheless, the new curriculum was not without its critics among the student body. To be sure, the teaching of mathematics, history and rhetoric by notable professors like Colin McLaurin, Charles Mackie and John Stevenson won general praise. But these were not part of the core curriculum and it was this that attracted criticism from an interesting and important section of the student population. Those with better educational backgrounds found the teaching of Latin and Greek rudimentary and many found the philosophy teaching pedestrian compared to the glamorous and innovative teaching that Francis Hutcheson was offering at Glasgow. Ambitious young divinity students like Alexander Carlyle, who longed for an 'improved' kirk run by a well-educated, gentlemanly clergy, found the divinity teaching 'dull, Dutch and prolix'. Restless, philosophically minded young lawyers like Henry Home complained that the teaching of civil law was dull and lacked the historical sparkle that advanced jurists were able to bring to the subject on the continent. Bright medical students like William Cullen complained that their professors did little more than recycle the lectures they had heard at Leiden. For the new curriculum seemed better suited to the needs of the country clergy, law clerks and surgeon's apprentices than to ambitious, philosophically minded professional gentlemen.

Perhaps the most conspicuous weakness of the reformed

curriculum lay in the teaching of moral philosophy. This, after all, was supposed to be the course which pulled the arts curriculum together by discussing the principles of morals and natural theology and by teaching students heading for the kirk, the professions and public life the meaning of virtue and public service in a Protestant state. But it was not until Ferguson's appointment in 1764 that the town council was able to find a professor who was able to satisfy them. The first three professors, William Law, William Scott and Sir John Pringle, who, between them, held the chair from 1708 to 1745, had completely different outlooks on their task and were conspicuously unable to generate much student interest, Law being more of a theologian, Scott being more of a classicist and a natural jurist, and Pringle being a physician who had eventually to be removed from the chair for absenteeism – though this did not prevent him from eventually becoming a distinguished President of the Royal Society. By 1745, the town council knew exactly what it wanted: the sort of teaching Francis Hutcheson was offering at Glasgow. Hutcheson, a Scots-Irish graduate of Glasgow, had been appointed to the moral philosophy chair at Glasgow in 1729 and had revolutionised the teaching of the subject by developing a new radical Whig account of the principles of morals, justice, politics and natural religion. As well as being an important philosopher, Hutcheson was a charismatic teacher and the town council cannot have failed to notice that ambitious Edinburgh students like Alexander Carlyle were travelling to Glasgow to hear him, even though Glasgow regrettably lacked 'a certain manner and address that can only be attained in the capital'. When the chair became vacant in 1745, the town council did the obvious thing and offered it to Hutcheson, who refused it. Then something curious and unfortunate happened. Edinburgh's most brilliant ex-student, David Hume applied for the chair, backed by some powerful sponsors. It would have been an extraordinary appointment. Hume's interest in moral philosophy was profound and original and he had an acute sense of its importance for public life. He was also deeply inter-

David Hume, from an
engraving by W. Holl,
after Allan Ramsay.
Scotland's greatest
philosopher had
attended classes at the
college and never
occupied a chair. But
his sceptical philosophy
greatly influenced
teaching in the
college during the
Enlightenment.
(Edinburgh University
Library, Special
Collections)

ested in communicating his philosophy to a large audience. The trouble was that he was a religious sceptic of the utmost power and brilliance and the prospect of his appointment shocked the kirk and indeed Francis Hutcheson, who played an important part in blocking it.

Instead the chair went to Pringle's former assistant, William Cleghorn, a radical Whig and a decent political philosopher with a limited interest in moral philosophy. Cleghorn held the chair until 1754, by which time Hume was a prominent and influential figure in Edinburgh's intellectual circles and the *bête noire* of the orthodox clergy. Although there was no question of appointing him, the kirk was determined to ensure that something was done to stem the spread of Humean scepticism. The new professor, James Balfour, fitted the bill perfectly. He was a lawyer and an orthodox Presbyterian who was willing to use his chair to defend the faith, a task he performed conscientiously enough to an ever-dwindling student audience. As William Robertson put it, it was 'a cruel loss to the country' that this all-important chair should have fallen into such hands. Indeed, it was a sign of the times that some thought the chair should be consigned to the faculty of divinity.

By 1745 the college was at an interesting stage of its development. The reforms Carstares and the town council had set in motion were more or less complete. The town council now had a college capable of teaching a 'Dutch' system of education competently, without any particular distinction, to respectable numbers of students. It was still very much the *Tounis* College, still governed academically, financially and administratively by a town council that was generally suspicious of any professorial attempt to take control of routine college business. Effective management of college business depended largely on relations between the Principal and the Lord Provost, and it was important to the success of the reform process that Carstares and Wishart were able to establish excellent relations with the provost, and notably with the college's great supporter, George Drummond.

But reform had only been possible because of the relationships that the college had established with the professional corporations and government. The development of the law and medical faculties had been a collaborative venture on the part of the town council and the Faculty of Advocates, the Surgeons' Incorporation and the College of Physicians, an arrangement that gave these corporations an important say in filling chairs and shaping curricula. Indeed, before 1767, the medical faculty developed as a semi-autonomous unit within the college, creating its own curriculum and its own regulations in its own way and in its own time. In the same way, although the Edinburgh presbytery had no comparable rights of patronage, it could often be articulate and effective in expressing its views on professorial appointments – as Hume had found to his cost.

But over and above these local corporate influences, lay the crown and the Earl of Ilay, the future Duke of Argyll. Carstares' reforms would have been impossible without the support of government. His excellent contacts at court had resulted in the grant of £300 per annum, which boosted general funds and paid for the Regius Chair of Public Law. Government support was where the future lay. Between 1703 and 1807 the crown founded nine Regius chairs, and provided a series of important grants for buildings, scientific instruments and general purposes. Indeed, without this patronage it is hard to see how the college could have entered its golden years later in the century. Inevitably this turned the college into a model of Whig political correctness, always ready with loyal addresses to the crown on state occasions, always attentive to the opinions and wishes of ministers when there were chairs to be filled. It is a sobering paradox that while Oxford and Cambridge slumbered intellectually throughout the period of enlightenment in a state of relative academic freedom, the politically obsequious Edinburgh excelled and became the model of an enlightened university.

All of this had a profound effect on the character and culture of the college. Professors and students were as notable for the parts they played in city life as for their academic activities. The professors generally had second lives as ministers, lawyers, physicians and surgeons mingling with fellow professionals and with men of rank and property as well as with their academic brethren. Clubs like the Rankenian Club, which flourished from 1717 to the Forty-Five and the Medical Society (later the Philosophical Society and later still the Royal Society of Edinburgh), which was founded in 1731 and flourished for the rest of the century, drew town and gown together in the interests of encouraging the improvement of learning and manners. As the Rankenian's historian put it, 'liberal conversation and rational enquiry' tended to encourage 'boldness of disquisition, liberality of sentiment, accuracy of reasoning, correctness of taste and attention to composition'. It was this, he thought, which had done so much to establish 'the exalted rank which Scotsmen hold at present [1774] in the republic of letters'. Professors were beginning to see themselves as scholars and gentlemen as well as college teachers, and the best of them, Monro, McLaurin and Stevenson, were beginning to see themselves as men of affairs with significant public roles to perform. They were to be the forerunners of the professoriate of the Robertson era.

The student body developed in much the same way as the professoriate, sometimes with their open help and connivance. In the 1720s the young Henry Home joined a 'Society for improving classical lore' to help make good the deficiencies of his classical education. By 1724 the young David Hume had become a member of the Physiological Library, which met with the active encouragement of the professor to discuss natural philosophy. The student's Medical Society, which was founded in 1737, was more ambitious, launching a critique of the Boerhaavian system of medical science, which was being taught by their professors. In the 1730s trendy, polite-minded divinity students founded a society to cultivate the art of public speaking so as to learn how they could preach as gentlemen rather than as traditional preachers. The college may not have had the buildings and dormitories that were characteristic of the other Scottish universities. What it did have was an academic community whose life and work was becoming integrated into the social and professional life of the city.

What was lacking in this period was the sense of collegiate identity that Glasgow and the Aberdeen colleges had and

This portrait of the Queen Regent, Mary of Guise, attributed to Corneille de Lyon, was painted in 1558, two years after she endowed two royal lectureships, in canon and civil law and in Greek. (Scottish National Portrait Gallery)

A heraldic window, one of very few surviving examples of pre-Reformation stained glass in Scotland, showing a roundel with the arms of Mary of Guise – a shield surmounted by a crown encircled by laurel – on the south wall of the Chapel of Mary Magdalen in Edinburgh's Cowgate, founded in 1547. The chapel was the venue where the Queen Regent's two royal lecturers gave their public lectures. (Scottish Reformation Society and Crown copyright: RCAHMS)

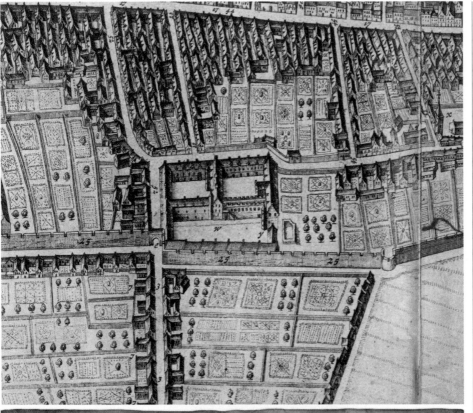

This bird's-eye view of
Old College is part of
the detailed map of
Edinburgh in 1647 by
James Gordon of
Rothiemay. It shows
three neat courtyards
surrounded by regular
ranges of college
buildings, including the
recently built library,
and the college garden
beyond. No. 52 on the
plan is Horse Wynd,
which led to the
Potterrow Port (e) and
no. 54 is College Wynd.
(The Trustees of the
National Library
of Scotland)

The Charter of the
University, dated 14
April 1582, which
confirmed grants of land
made to the 'tounis
college' by Mary, Queen
of Scots in 1567. Less
a foundation charter
than an enabling one,
it was issued by the
privy council.
(Courtesy of
Edinburgh City
Archives)

A fine portrait, formerly attributed to Sir Antony Van Dyck on the basis of its quality, of Alexander Henderson (1583–1646), minister of Edinburgh, co-author of the National Covenant (1638) and Rector of the College (1640–6). Henderson's period saw a loan of £21,777 Scots raised, new professors appointed and the beginning of building of the new library (Scottish National Portrait Gallery)

Prof. James Gregory (1638–75), a chalk drawing by the 11th Earl of Buchan after John Scougall. Professor of Mathematics at St Andrews (1670) and at Edinburgh (1674) for a short time before his early death, Gregory was the first of a new breed of highly paid professors outside the traditional dominant subject of theology. His duties amounted to two public lectures a week. (Scottish National Portrait Gallery)

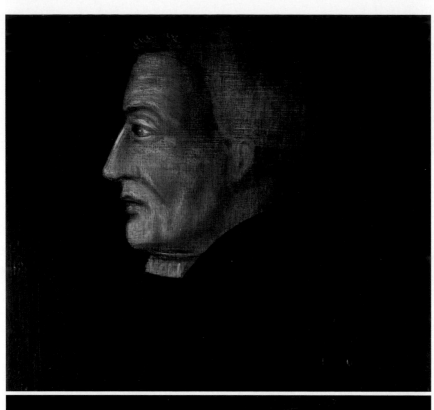

The university had a collection of portraits of Protestant reformers, beginning with Martin Luther. Here are those of Martin Bucer, reformer of Strasbourg (top left); Theodore Beza, Rector of the Academy in Calvin's Geneva (bottom left); and George Buchanan, tutor to James VI (right). One of the pretexts for dismissing Alexander Monro as Principal in the purge of staff in 1690 was the fact that he had removed these portraits from display in the Upper Library Hall. (Edinburgh University Library, Special Collections)

A fine, official royal binding, stamped 'Jacobus 6 Rex Scotorum' with a crown imperial, adorns this Greek textbook, published in 1568, which was later given as a bequest to the library. (Edinburgh University Library, Special Collections)

William Carstares, Principal (1703–15), by William Aikman. Carstares remodelled the classics and philosophy curriculum on Dutch lines. (Talbot Rice Gallery, University of Edinburgh)

Francis Hutcheson, by Allan Ramsay. Professor of Moral Philosophy at Glasgow (1729–46), Hutcheson was the so-called 'Father of the Scottish Enlightenment'. (© Hunterian Art Gallery, University of Glasgow)

Archibald Campbell, Earl of Ilay and 3rd Duke of Argyll, by Allan Ramsay. The so-called 'Uncrowned King of Scotland' from around 1725 to 1761, he was a cultured and powerful nobleman who exercised a profound influence on university appointments. (Scottish National Portrait Gallery)

Edinburgh would acquire later in the century. There was no constitution to give the professors control over their own business, notoriously inadequate buildings and no independent source of income. All that kept the system together was whatever personal authority the Principal could exert over his faculty. From 1736 to 1753, Principal Wishart tried to establish some sort of discipline within the college by visiting classes, supervising the examination of students and delivering college addresses and sermons. His successor, the elderly Principal Gowdie, however, was not so energetic. From 1753 to 1762, the Senatus never met and Gowdie was content to leave the professors to their own devices. It was a situation that his successor, Principal Robertson, would address with conspicuous success in the wake of the momentous upheaval in the cultural life of the city that followed the Forty-Five.

The Forty-Five was a watershed in the history of the country, the city and the college. When news reached Edinburgh that the Pretender's army was marching on the city, the Court of Session adjourned, the banks ceased trading, leading citizens hastily left for the country and college classes were suspended. There were no Jacobites among the professoriate and few if any student sympathisers; indeed, the college was notable for its loyalism. Colin McLaurin worked feverishly to improve the city's fortifications and suffered a fatal stroke in consequence. Charles Mackie infected the town with spurious scare stories about Jacobite atrocities. The college formed its own company of volunteers which the young William Robertson and a number of young divinity students joined, a horrified Principal Wishart imploring them not to fight lest 'the flower of the youth of Edinburgh' should be mown down.

The Forty-Five brought home the political realities of the Union in no uncertain terms; power now lay with London and there was little or nothing that Scots could do about it. It was an experience that galvanised the political thinking of a new generation of lawyers, ministers and men of letters who were to dominate the cultural life of Edinburgh for the rest of the century. These were men who had been born in the 1720s and had grown up in a city that was becoming an important centre of government and politics. They had been educated in Edinburgh's 'Dutch' college and had cast envious eyes at the new system of education being developed at Glasgow. By 1745 they were beginning to find their professional feet and were asking what was expected of them as patriots and citizens of a modern British state. It was a question they would attempt to answer by turning to the cultivation of their own minds and to public education. They wanted professional men to think about their professions in philosophical as well as practical terms and to see themselves as gentlemen as well as patriots. They wanted to cultivate the outlook on public life that was already characteristic of Hutcheson's Glasgow and would eventually characterise Robertson's Edinburgh.

During the sixteen years between Culloden and Robertson's appointment as Principal, it was the city rather than the college that was to be the laboratory of this new generation's approach to culture. It was a period which saw a startling proliferation of clubs and societies dedicated to the improvement of philosophy, letters and public life. None was more important than the Select Society (1754–?63), which was mostly composed of the younger ministers, lawyers, doctors and men of letters and an impressive array of peers and landed gentlemen. The Select Society debated questions about the principles of law, morality, politics and the fine arts and the problem of generating political, economic and cultural improvement in a modern state. It organised elaborate schemes for encouraging practical improvement in the arts and sciences. It was a programme that made the Select Society the focal point of the city's cultural life and the institutional embodiment of its claim to be a centre of enlightenment. It is significant that many of the future professors of the Robertson era were members. But perhaps the most striking and durable statement of this spirit of improvement and enlightenment is to be found in the *Proposals for carrying on certain Public Works in the*

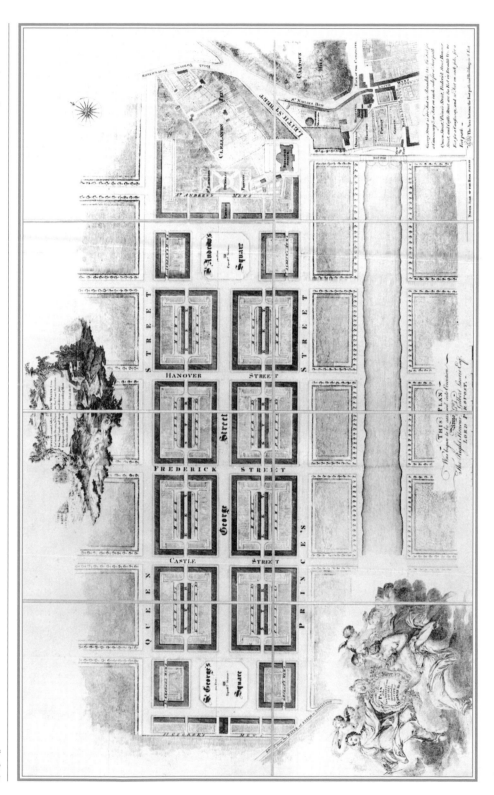

James Craig, 'Plan of the new streets and squares intended for the City of Edinburgh, 1767'. (Courtesy of Edinburgh City Libraries)

The Ceremony of laying the Foundation Stone of the New College of Edinburgh, 16 November 1789. Lord Napier, Grand Master Mason of Scotland, lays the foundation stone of the new college. He faces Principal Robertson and the professors. (University of Edinburgh)

City of Edinburgh of 1752, the blueprint for a regenerated city with new public buildings and a new residential suburb, the modern New Town. The *Proposals* were the work of Lord Provost George Drummond, the town council and the professional corporations. However, the language in which they were written was the language of the Select Society, the language of enlightened Edinburgh. The *Proposals* speak of a dirty, decrepit city rarely visited by the nobility or foreigners, a city still beset by 'local prejudices and narrow notions, inconsistent with polished manners and growing wealth'. They looked forward to the time when a redeveloped city '[would] naturally become the centre of trade and commerce, of learning and the arts, of politeness and refinement of every kind'. And they saw the responsibility for bringing about this great change as being theirs and theirs alone. 'At no period surely did there ever appear a more general, or a better directed zeal for the improvement and prosperity of this country. Persons of every rank and denomination seem at length to be actuated by a truly public and national spirit.' 'What,' the *Proposals* asked '[can] prove more beneficial to SCOTLAND, and by consequence to UNITED BRITAIN?'

For all its modest educational strengths, it was clear that the spirit of much of the college's teaching was out of step with these enlightened ideals. To be sure, in the medical faculty professors like Robert Whytt, Professor of the Theory and Practice of Medicine from 1747 to 1766, Alexander Monro II, Professor of Anatomy from 1754 to 1798, and William Cullen, poached from Glasgow in 1755 as Professor of Chemistry from 1755 to 1766 and thereafter Professor of the Institutes of Medicine from 1766 to 1790, were laying the foundation stones of the practical and philosophical curriculum that was to give the Edinburgh medical school its international reputation. What is more, their approach to medical education seemed to be attracting significant numbers of students; by the 1750s there were about 300 medical students, half the size of the student body as a whole, and the number was rising.

The real problem lay in developing this culture in other

faculties – a problem in which the Lord Provost, George Drummond, the Duke of Argyll and his successor as the government's Scottish 'manager' in the early 1760s were greatly interested. Their aim was to draw the educational culture of the college into alignment with the culture of an enlightened city by promoting leading members of the young moderate clergy like William Robertson, Hugh Blair and Adam Ferguson. These were rapidly earning formidable reputations as ministers, scholars and men of affairs. During the 1750s they successfully defended the hated institution of lay patronage in the General Assembly and they defended three of the leading members of the *literati*, David Hume, Lord Kames and the playwright John Home, against charges of heterodoxy. In so doing, they managed to establish a tight grip on the government of the kirk, which they maintained for the next generation. At the same time they were establishing themselves as leaders of the Select Society and as important patrons of learning and letters. They were ripe for promotion. The Duke of Argyll took the first step in 1759 by securing the appointment of Adam Ferguson to the chair of natural philosophy, on the understanding that it was to be a stepping stone to the all-important chair of moral philosophy. In 1762 the new prime minister, the Earl of Bute, persuaded the king to found a Regius chair of rhetoric and belles lettres for Hugh Blair on the grounds that public interest in the subject was such that the new chair would 'bring additional numbers of Schollars to the College'. But the greatest catch was William Robertson who was appointed Principal in 1762 on the death of John Gowdie. It was an appointment that was to have profound consequences for the college.

In 1762 Robertson was thirty-nine and had already established himself as the undisputed leader of the polite moderates. He was a minister's son who had attended the college between 1733 and c. 1741 and was destined for the kirk. Like so many students of that generation, he seems to have learned more from the study of history and rhetoric than from the core content of the arts and divinity curricula. The oratory and the political skills he showed in the General Assembly in defending patronage and the theologically suspect *literati* were greatly admired in Edinburgh and London, and even won the respect of some of his opponents. He was also attracting attention as a leading member of the *literati* and a prominent member of the Select Society. The seal was set on his intellectual and political reputation in 1759 when he published what is still one of the most original and controversial histories of Scotland. The prime minister tried to persuade him to move to London so that he could write a new history of England, but Robertson preferred Edinburgh. He was richly rewarded with a royal chaplaincy and the post of Historiographer Royal and his presentation to Greyfriars' church was easily managed. Gowdie's death in 1762 opened the way to the principalship. Robertson realise that the job would not be as rewarding as the life of a London-based government pensioner, but 'it is the situation rather than any increase of Salary that is my object'. Rich, well-connected, admired, ambitious and young, he was by far the most formidable Principal the college had ever had and was to leave indelible marks on its history.

Robertson lost no time in stamping his authority on the college. Working with the Lord Provost, George Drummond, he got rid of his principal opponent, the Professor of Ecclesiastical History, Patrick Cuming. He reactivated the Senatus Academicus and set it to work reforming the degree structure and the curriculum. He took steps to integrate the administration of the medical faculty into the general administration of the college. He persuaded the town council and the crown to invest in the college and, particularly, to develop the potential of the medical faculty. New professorships were established in pharmacology (1768), surgery (1777), natural history (1790), astronomy (1790) and agriculture (1790). The chair of botany was turned into a Regius chair and the professor, John Hope, was given a new botanical garden in 1763 paid for by the crown. The library – Robertson's particular interest – was extended, refitted and refinanced by the town council and a new natural history museum was built. The college's

crumbling building stock was extensively repaired and refitted. As we shall see, Robertson's most grandiose project, a new college building to replace the old, paid for by a public subscription, was to prove more problematical. Robertson managed all of this with surprisingly little opposition from his colleagues – it was said that the Senatus never voted. It is even more surprising that from 1762 to 1778 there was virtually no interference on the part of the town council or the government in the running of the college or the filling of vacant chairs – and this in spite of the fact that the town council had always been touchy about its status as the College's patrons. Indeed, in a striking moment in 1772, Lord Provost Gilbert Lawrie formally acknowledged that the college had now acquired a quasi-corporate status by addressing the Senatus as 'the Faculty of the College'.

What set the seal on Robertson's administration were his

appointments. Between 1762 and 1793 every single chair became vacant, sometimes more than once. Such was Robertson's formidable standing with the Senatus, the town council and the government that all but a handful went to his nominees; indeed, it was only in the 1780s, when his health was failing, that his influence showed signs of waning. At one level, Robertson's professoriate was a very eighteenth-century affair, a network of cronies and kinsmen who generally had the crucial advantage of being polite Presbyterians. Yet, academically, it was, on the whole, an extraordinarily distinguished oligarchy. Stars like Adam Ferguson, Dugald Stewart and Hugh Blair, William Cullen, Joseph Black, Alexander Monro II, John Hope and John Gregory won international reputations as teachers of philosophy and medicine. Less dramatically, Robertson's administration saw the appointment of professors of law, divinity and the classics whose teaching fitted the polite

Presbyterian ideal of approaching subjects philosophically, or as critics sometimes put it, 'metaphysically'.

In fact it was this approach to university teaching that did much to establish the university's international reputation as an 'enlightened' university. Throughout the university, students were encouraged to study phenomena in terms of the general principles they illustrated and it was not uncommon for professors in all disciplines to draw ethical and theological conclusions from their teaching. It was teaching designed to encourage students to think about their place in the natural and moral world, about the nature of the Deity who superintended it, and about the duties they owed to the Deity and the public. To be sure, things worked out differently in different faculties and with different professors. In the arts faculty, Ferguson's and Dugald Stewart's teaching was heavily moralised and directed to political life and was widely admired for being so. In the medical faculty, celebrated and charismatic professors like Alexander Monro II and 'the great and unrivalled' William Cullen were sometimes criticised for dealing too much 'upon theory' and for not paying enough attention to the 'demonstrative' side of their subjects. What is more, as medical students sometimes found to their cost, the different 'systems' they were taught by their professors often bore little obvious relationship to each other. Indeed, as Michael Barfoot has put it, by the end of Robertson's administration, the medical curriculum had become more like an overgrown plantation than a carefully cultivated Georgian landscape garden. Nevertheless, as many parents realised, there was no other university in Britain and few anywhere else 'where every branch of science is regularly taught and drawn together so compactly from one to the other'.

The success of this approach to education was gratifyingly evident in the number of students the college began to attract from at home and abroad. By the mid-1760s there were around 600 students, half of whom were studying medicine, making Edinburgh the largest university in Scotland. By the time of Robertson's death in 1793, there were 751 matriculated students, 427 of whom were medicals. But these figures only tell part of the story. In spite of periodic attempts to tighten up the formal qualifications needed for graduation, those who did not want or need a degree did not matriculate and simply enrolled in the courses of their choice and paid the professor the appropriate fee. The first meeting of a class was always devoted to paying fees directly and in cash to the professor; Joseph Black even took the precaution of weighing the coins in which he was paid. Generally speaking, arts students only bothered to matriculate if they were heading for the divinity faculty or were proposing to teach; medical students only did so if they were aiming at an Edinburgh degree; the large and expanding number of English, Irish, American and European medical students generally reckoned to complete their courses and graduate in London or Paris. In the law faculty, matriculation and graduation were unknown.

In spite of valuable recent work on the medical faculty, far too little is known about the composition of the student body during the Robertson era. Nevertheless, it was clearly remarkably heterogeneous. Many of the Scots seem to have been law clerks, surgeons' apprentices and country boys often from poor backgrounds who were heading for Divinity Hall and careers as ministers and parish schoolmasters. Divinity students generally studied classics and philosophy before entering Divinity Hall. Clerks and apprentices were more likely to do what their masters told them, although the more fortunate would be encouraged to attend classics, philosophy and chemistry classes. It was the better-off students from Scotland and abroad who were the most likely to lead the classic life of the enlightened student, spending their free time in taverns, debating societies and, maybe at the theatre, in assemblies or at the summer races at Leith. They might even study the fine arts and modern languages with private tutors. There was likely to be a qualitative difference in the sort of education rich and poorer students received. The poorer classics and philosophy students received most of their education in large 'public' classes and while professors would probably spend one of their weekly lecture hours going over their lectures, there was, as critics frequently pointed out, not much opportunity for the closer quasi-tutorial contact that richer students could gain from the professor's private classes or that very rich students got by boarding with the professor and receiving private supervision from him. Samuel Baird, one of Cullen's students in 1764, wrote home lyrically about the great chemist's private classes:

> We convene at his own house once or twice a week, where after lecturing for one hour, we spend another in an easy conversation upon the subject of the last evening's lecture, & every one is encouraged to make his remarks or objections with the greatest freedom & ease – I cannot help comparing him upon these occasions to *Socrates* or some other of the ancient philosophers surrounded by his admiring pupils.

In the end, you got what you paid for. By the 1790s it was reckoned that £10 per quarter or £20 for the winter session was the least one could pay 'to live in a genteel manner' and there were fees to be paid on top of that; poor students clearly lived on very much less. It was a system of education which had the effect of privileging the wealthy and those who had access to political power. At the same time it offered a sophisticated general education to able boys from humble backgrounds who could be expected to perform useful social roles at lower levels of society. It was typical of the spirit of this system that professors were generally good talent-spotters who were willing to let the best of the poorer students join their private classes free and gain an entry to the world of opportunity and advancement.

During his thirty years' administration Robertson not only turned the university into one of the most important universities in the western world, but succeeded in placing it at the centre of the cultural life of the city. It was only natural that he should have wanted to immortalise his achievement in new buildings. At the time of his appointment, the college's build-

ings were generally seen as a disgrace, 'hae miseriae nostrae' as
he called them. Nevertheless they typified the distinctive relationship that the college had developed with the city. The
college was situated where it now is, at Kirk O' Fields. The
three-acre site formed a quadrangle with a college garden and
a hugger-mugger site of oddly assorted and poorly maintained
old buildings, many of which were not even used for college
purposes. Some were let out to teachers, others to tradesmen
and even, a shocked Victorian historian exclaimed, to a coal
merchant. The garden accommodated the physic garden and
was overlooked by the College of Surgeons and the 'elabora-
tory' built by the four founders of the medical faculty to
develop and market their medicines.

Robertson had opened his campaign for a brand-new
college building in 1768 with a *Memorial Relating to Edinburgh
University*. This breathed the same spirit as the *Proposals* of 1752.

Edinburgh now had what Robertson described as a flourishing *university,* consisting of 21 professors and 600–700 students and 'a course of Academical education as complete as any Univer-sity of Europe'. (It is significant that Robertson never used the term 'College', let alone 'Tounis College'.) It was 'much resorted to by the nobility and gentry of this part of the country' and was now, Robertson observed, rather optimistically, attracting students 'from all parts of Britain, from Ireland, America, the West Indies and even from distant parts of Europe'. In a city famed for its love of improvement, 'the University fabric alone remains in such a neglected state as to be generally accounted a dishonour to the city of Edinburgh and to this part of the Country'. Hinting that the needs of the University had now outgrown the resources of the town council, the Principal called for an entirely new building with 'a Public Hall, a Library, a Musaeum and convenient Teaching Rooms for the several Professors'. It would cost £15,000 and would be funded by public subscription.

Robertson's plan was over ambitious. The subscription was launched and failed and the plan had to be shelved for twenty years. But the town council's plans for the development of the south side of the city inevitably raised questions about the future of the college site. An enormous bridge linking the High Street to the new Register House had been opened in 1772 and the town council was now preparing to extend the development southwards, over the Cowgate, through the existing site of the college and onwards to Newington and the south. It was a *grand projet* creating opportunities for a major new exercise in town planning and it was one which greatly interested the celebrated architect, Robert Adam, an alumnus of the College, a former member of the Select Society and the Principal's cousin.

Adam saw the new street as a spacious avenue which would be flanked by grand colonnaded terraces of shops and apartments and a magnificently developed college site. On the north-west side of the avenue would be a triumphal arch, which would serve as the entrance to a new college building.

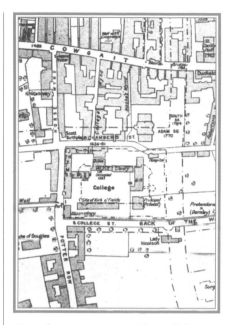

This reconstruction of the college and its environs by Henry F. Kerr is superimposed on the Ordnance Survey map of Edinburgh in 1851, shown by dotted lines. (from *Book of the Old Edinburgh Club*, Original Series XI (1922), pp. 1–19; courtesy of the Old Edinburgh Club)

On the opposite side of the street, the avenue would take the form of a crescent of professorial houses, interspersed with an assembly room, a concert hall, a coffee-house and a book shop. The new avenue was to house an academic suburb epitomising learning and politeness and the civic values of an enlightened city. Adam's visionary plan never left the drawing-board. It was too expensive and there were too many rival architects and builders with different ideas, all anxious for a share of the action. But the future of the college site was becoming urgent and Adam's plan for a new building with a magnificent facade on the South Bridge resurfaced in 1789. Once again, Robertson seems to have played a decisive part in taking the project forward. Adam was his choice as architect and the Senatus seems to have taken the lead in providing him with specifications for the new building.

Adam's plans were characteristically grandiose. The new college was to be composed of two courtyards, four storeys high with a great colonnaded entrance on the South Bridge. It was to contain public lecture rooms and private rooms for the professors, a library, a museum and a great hall; controversially, there was to be no chapel. There was to be a suite of rooms to house the new Royal Society of Edinburgh and to reinforce

Adam saw the new college buildings as part of an academic enclave that would be approached from the Register House by means of an avenue of the utmost grandeur.

TOP
Perspective view over South Bridge.

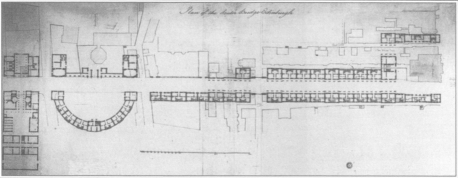

MIDDLE
Plan of South Bridge, original scheme, 1785.

BOTTOM
Triumphal arch for entrance to the college, 1785.

(Illustrations by kind permission of the Trustees of Sir John Soane's Museum, London)

the new college's claim to be the focal point of the cultural life of the city. There was to be another suite of rooms to house the grandest of student societies, the Speculative Society. There were to be four professorial mansions, though no accommodation for students, these last, Professor John Gregory observed, '[living] promiscuously with the other inhabitants of the city'. It was to be the largest and most magnificent public building in Scotland and was to cost around £63,000. Adam expected it to be 'a monument of my talents'.

Adam and Robertson saw the project in national terms. The new college was to be paid for by subscription from the nobility, gentry, professional corporations and the royal burghs as well as by contributions from the town council and government. The foundation stone was laid on 16 November 1789 by the Master Mason of Scotland, Lord Napier, in a ceremony of great magnificence, attended by 'upward of 300 noblemen and gentlemen' and watched by a crowd of 30,000. In his speech Robertson once again declared that the college had become a national institution. It was 'a seat of education to youth in every part of the British dominions' and to 'almost every nation in Europe and every state in America'. It was 'a mansion of science' designed 'to instill into the minds of youth principles of sound knowledge, to inspire them with the love of religion and virtue, and prepare them for filling the various stations in society with honour to themselves, and with benefit to their country'. The new college was a project which had always been the object of Robertson's 'warmest wishes'. It would be the epitome of the spirit of the Scottish Enlightenment. The only sour note at the ceremony was the medical students complaining that they had not been invited to the party.

Robertson's and Adam's plan for the new college took shape quickly. The initial response to the appeal was encouraging – by 1791 more than £18,000 had been subscribed from the crown, the city, the legal and medical corporations, from the bulk of the nobility and from doctors and lawyers, and by 1797 the total had risen to around £30,000. Building had proceeded apace. By 1793 the north-west corner of the new college,

FRIENDSHIP.

A principal Beard.

THE ELDER SHALL SERVE THE YOUNGER

Rom IX ver I

I Kay fecit 1793

which housed the anatomy theatre, was complete and work on the façade had begun. Adam died suddenly in 1792; Robertson died after years of illness, a year later. In their last months it must have seemed possible that the great work would be accomplished. But then it all started going wrong.

Robertson was succeeded in 1793 by the Professor of Divinity, George Husband Baird, a bearded nonentity whose sole qualification for the office was that he was the Lord Provost's son-in-law. Nevertheless, it was a significant appointment. Faced with the escalating costs of the new building, the town council was determined to tighten its grip on the management of the college by appointing a principal it could rely on. It was to usher in a period of tense and sometimes acrimonious relations between town and gown that lasted until the constitutional link between them was finally broken in 1858.

The problem of completing the new building and paying for it was to dominate college business until the 1830s. At the time of Robertson's death the public subscription had

The half-built college,
from an engraving by
Lizars and Basire, 1823.

produced only £30,000 – less than half of what was needed.
The town council had little option but to turn to government.
However, war with France until 1815 meant that the government had other financial priorities to attend to. Work on the
building stopped abruptly in 1794, less than a quarter having
been completed and new buildings under construction being
left unroofed and unfinished. The college had become little
more than a building site, old buildings jostling with new, 'a
melancholy memorial of ill-judged haste in its commence-
ment' as one visitor put it. As the Senatus commented, it was
ironical that students were now faced with 'greater inconven-
iences than were felt during the miserable state of the old
buildings'. By the end of the war, it was clear that the entire
project would have to be rethought. It was now reckoned that
it would cost around £150,000 to finish Adam's building at a
time when the college's annual income was no more than
£9,000 and less than the amount needed to pay the cost of
salaries and bursaries. It was the great achievement of the Lord

The Upper Museum, from an engraving by W. H. Lizars, c.1822. The Museum became one of Edinburgh's leading tourist attractions. Note the tame puma.

Provost, Sir John Marjoribanks, to persuade the government to pay for the completion of a scaled-down project. A government commission was set up to manage the project and £10,000 per annum for seven years was set aside to pay for it. The British state had stepped in to take over a project that was beyond the reach of the enlightened patriotic Scottish public, on which Robertson had hoped to rely.

The appointment of the 25-year-old William Playfair as architect to the new project was something of a masterstroke. Not only was he a disciple of Adam, he was able to get on with the commissioners, the town council and the professors. The professors knew him of old – he was one of them, the nephew of the Professor of Natural Philosophy as well as an alumnus. Playfair, for his part, understood very well what was needed. He proposed replacing Adam's two courts with a single, large quadrangle. Adam's contentious plans for a graduation hall, professorial houses and accommodation for the Royal Society of Edinburgh were scrapped. So were his plans for a dome over the eastern facade. New plans were drawn up for a natural history museum and library, both of the utmost magnificence – a move that met with universal approval.

Indeed the only serious opposition to the plan came from

the divinity faculty, which once again complained about the lack of a chapel. Building started in 1817 and was more or less completed by 1827, after repeated requests for more money from an increasingly irritable Treasury. It was not until 1832 and only then after a final appeal for money to lay out the court-yard that the building was more or less complete. It had proved to be a less heroic, less patriotic enterprise than Robertson and Adam had intended, but it was still a magnificent monument to a Whig–Liberal British state.

In spite of its building problems the college continued to expand. Student numbers expanded dramatically between the 1790s and 1820s, the number of matriculated students almost tripling between 1791 and 1825, from 757 to 2,013, and the estimated numbers of non-matriculating students making short visits to the college bringing the total number of students to around 1,300 in 1799 and 2,000 in 1815. It was a student population which continued to be dominated by medical students, who constituted around 60 per cent of the matriculated population in 1810 and 44 per cent in the later 1820s. It was also gratifyingly cosmopolitan. During the period of the wars with France, it was estimated that about a third of the medical students came from England, Ireland and the colonies and elsewhere, their numbers dropping in the post-war years as new medical schools and universities opened up in Europe and America and as Edinburgh's medical reputation began to sag. Although these foreign students were generally non-matriculating and non-graduating students who spent a limited amount of time at the university, they were among the most likely to connect with the Robertsonian ideal of combining practical and philosophical education by attending classes in natural and moral philosophy and chemistry as well as in medicine. In fact, they were treating the university exactly as the Scots had treated Leiden and Utrecht a century before, as a cosmopolitan centre of learning that was able to provide them with the sort of education which was not available at home. Furthermore, just as Dutch education had once played a formative role in shaping the Edinburgh curriculum, so the Edinburgh curriculum was to play a historic part in reshaping European and American university education in the post-war years.

The faculty was still a force to be reckoned with. New Regius chairs in clinical and military surgery and in medical jurisprudence were founded between 1803 and 1807. A chair of conveyancing was founded in collaboration with the Society of Writers to the Signet in 1825. There was a new generation of professorial stars like the Professor of Natural Philosophy, John Playfair, the Professor of Mathematics, Sir John Leslie, and the Professor of Chemistry, T. C. Hope, who were able to attract international as well as local attention. Indeed, for a time Hope was probably the most important chemistry teacher in Europe, his huge – and lucrative – classes of 500 or more and his spectacular demonstrations turning lecturing into a form of theatre which prompted his colleague John Leslie to call him 'the showman in the other corner'. Perhaps most striking of all was the explosion in the number of student debating societies, a mushroom growth which developed in all faculties and in all subjects. At their most basic, these provided a form of self-education, in which, as J. G. Lockhart observed, '[students] canvass at night the doctrines they have heard promulgated in the lecture of the morning'. At their most formal and sophisticated they continued to be the sort of rhetorical gymnasia the moderate professors of the Robertson era had so much admired. It was notable that Adam and Robertson's plans for housing the most august of them all, the Speculative Society, in the new college, survived Playfair's cutbacks.

Nevertheless there were difficulties which would have profound consequences for the future. The college was becoming increasingly oligarchic and prone to outside influence. Between 1786 and 1807 eight of the ten appointments to medical chairs were sons of professors and there was evidence of discrimination against Whigs. At the same time, many medical professors resented and resisted the founding of new chairs in a rapidly changing field for fear that it would erode their incomes. The kirk flexed its muscles in 1805 by attempting to block the appointment of Sir John Leslie to the mathematics chair for speaking of Hume with approval. Political interference was responsible for the appointment of a flashy, local journalist, John Wilson, to the all-important chair of moral philosophy in 1823, in spite of the fact that he knew no philosophy. David Masson remembered that 'in his class there was constant cheering of him on the least opportunity, especially by the juveniles of his audience, and yet with a kind of wondering respect for his reputation, voice and magnificent appearance, which kept the full sway really in his hands'.

The character of the student population was also changing in a way that had important consequences for the system of education. This was particularly noticeable in the medical faculty. The expansion of student numbers was a direct response to a rising public demand for trained medical men who might or might not have medical degrees. At the top end of the market there were good livings to be made in private practice by doctors who had the minds and manners of gentlemen. There was also a growing lower-level demand for doctors in the army, navy and in India and in country practice. Students with an eye on these less glamorous jobs provided the backbone of the faculty for most of the early nineteenth century.

William Borthwick's class tickets (1769–72), and (opposite) an Anatomy and Surgery class note (1785). At a time when few students matriculated or graduated, class tickets were the only evidence of attendance at university. They were consequently highly prized. (Edinburgh University Library, Special Collections)

Some matriculated, played a full part in student life and graduated. Many more were surgeons' apprentices, who spent most of the day working for their masters and taking the courses they were told to take. Most of them wanted a practical education and enough class notes to prove they had attended different courses to qualify them for membership of the college or for government service. To be sure, some of their masters had thoroughly enlightened views about their educational responsibilities and sent their apprentices to classes in Latin and Greek and natural and moral philosophy and chemistry as well as in medicine. What is more, some of them tutored their pupils on what they had heard in the college, underlining what many were beginning to think was the greatest weaknesses of the Edinburgh system, the lack of tutoring and testing. By the 1820s the college was becoming increasingly dependent on

semi-detached students, whose loyalties and educational expectations were controlled by professional corporations outside the college.

This had consequences for teaching and education. In the law faculty it was noticeable that 'philosophical' courses like public law and civil law were only attracting a handful of students destined for the bar and that the largest attendances were to be found in 'practical' classes like Scots law and, after 1825, conveyancing. Indeed, one witness giving evidence to the Royal Commission on the Universities in 1831 graphically underscored a fact of educational life which was as noticeable in the law faculty as in the faculty of medicine, that the majority of law student were law clerks. 'The mornings from an early hour, especially during the sittings of the Court, are not at the command of [most law students]; the evenings are devoted to

Within the sketch: *Civil Law Class 2d. Feb. 1819.*

hard labour, and the only part of the day which can be given to attendance on classes, is from two o'clock till four.'

In the case of the medical faculty the Royal Commission of 1825 noted that medical education was becoming increasingly practical and that professors were becoming increasingly cautious about the claims they were making about the nature and purpose of a medical education. The Dean, William Pultney Alison, denied that it was the job of the university to produce doctors who were scientists and gentlemen. 'No school of medicine can do more than give the elementary education upon which the character of each practitioner must be formed separately for himself.' He simply hoped that 'by the education we give him here, we trust that we afford to our graduates a greater facility of acquiring the character of skilful practitioners than they would otherwise have.' The trouble was that this practical education was becoming staid and open to criticism. Not only did many medical professors oppose the expansion of the faculty, they continued to teach by means of lectures and demonstrations without giving their students any

Student's sketch of the Civil Law classroom in 1819. (Edinburgh University Library, Special Collections)

practical experience of dissection, and experimentation and without providing any form of tutorial contact, things that could only be got from private teachers in the city and then only at a price.

At the heart of the college's problems lay its relations with the town council. Throughout the period, quarrels about buildings, finance and general administration continued to sour relations between town and gown. What brought matters to a head was a long-standing quarrel within the medical faculty over the question of which courses ought to be compulsory for graduation – a matter which affected class sizes and professorial incomes. This was undoubtedly a matter that lay within the town council's jurisdiction and its rights were eventually upheld by the Court of Session. The Senatus claimed that such matters were part of 'the essential and undefeasable nature and character of an University', and petitioned the crown to visit the college in the expectation that it would recommend severing the constitutional link between the town council and the university and placing its government in the hands of a university court. Visitors were appointed in 1825 to investigate the affairs of all of the Scottish universities – the first such visitation since the 1690s. But the Senatus' plans backfired. The visitors reviewed every area of college administration and teaching in meticulous detail. However, what really interested them was the system of education and it was to this that they devoted most of their time and attention. It has sometimes been said that this was a visitation of anglicisers bent on imposing an alien, classics-based system of university education on the Scottish system. There is something in this; the visitors were certainly deeply troubled by the lack of serious classical education in Scottish schools and universities. But it is probably better to think of the visitors as enlightened Scotsmen who valued order and system and were sensitive to the problems institutions faced in adjusting to the pressures created by the progress of society.

In the case of Edinburgh, what they found was a college with haphazard or non-existent arrangements for matriculation, registering class attendances and for examining students for graduation. They were worried by the backward state of classical education in Scottish schools and universities on the grounds that this was needed by those who wanted to play an active part in public life. They were troubled by the fact that the college seemed ill-equipped for turning out professional men who were scholars and gentlemen. The visitors' recommendations were Robertsonian in spirit but wholly impracticable and loaded with troubling social implications. It was thought that the college should only admit those who had passed an entrance examination in the classics and that it should aim at producing professional men who were scholars and gentlemen. It was a proposal which would have had the immediate effect of excluding many of the apprentices and clerks on whom the professors depended for their incomes and would have shut the door to most of the poor. Only after prompting did the visitors issue a supplementary report which recommended breaking the constitutional link between the university and the town council by establishing a rectorial court 'of intelligent and well-educated persons' to govern the university. But nothing happened. The early 1830s was an era of Whig reform and intense legislative activity and the parliamentary timetable was seriously congested and, anyway, the Senatus was prepared to put up with the inconvenience of remaining the Tounis College for the sake of ditching deeply unpalatable curricular changes. Until 1858, the college was to remain as it had always been: 'nothing more than a public and free school for instruction in the sciences and literature, with the single privilege of conferring academical degrees'. These were the bitter words of a Senatus that had tried and failed to turn the Tounis College into a university. It did not help that the town council marked its victory by appointing a general secretary to manage the college administration and to report on its affairs to his masters. It would be left to the Victorians to break the link between town and gown and to lay the constitutional foundations of the university we now know.

The publication of the commissioners' report in 1831

brought the most remarkable period in the history of the college to an end. The period had ended as it had begun with a radical investigation of the entire system of university education by the state. It had been a period in which the history of the college had been shaped by government, the town council and the professional corporations. It had seen the college and its system of education hi-jacked by orthodox Presbyterians in Rule's day, by an early generation of 'Dutch' Presbyterians in Carstares and by the polite, moderate Presbyterians in Robertson's. So, far from being the story of a steady progress towards enlightenment, it had been a story of radical make-overs, as one generation reacted to the legacy of another. And yet, in Robertson's day at least, it had worked. This unpromising constitutional and institutional system had generated a system of university education that was not only widely admired but was widely imitated throughout continental Europe and in America in the later eighteenth and early nineteenth centuries. It was the unique interplay between city and college, between a sense of the practical and the philosophical, between learning and public life in a city preoccupied with its own future that shaped the educational culture of the college in the 'Long Eighteenth Century'. It was that which had made it possible for the Tounis College to develop as an enlightened university.

PART III

The Construction of a Modern University

Robert D. Anderson

Battle of the Quadrangle

CHAPTER I

Age of Reform

Between the 1830s and the 1890s the university underwent a complex process of reform and adaptation, largely in response to outside pressures. As Scotland became more industrialised, more urban and more secular, an educational system rooted in a rural and religious society was transformed. The universities came under pressure to evolve in tune with national needs – 'national' meaning both Scottish and British. By their very nature, they produced an elite, though one with a much wider social base than at Oxford or Cambridge. That elite was expanding, and increasingly defined by the possession of formal educational qualifications. To the observer in the twenty-first century, the most surprising feature of the university in 1830 is perhaps the absence of examinations and the minor role of graduation. Today, we think of universities as, above all, the dispensers of professional qualifications. In the early nineteenth century, too, the university prepared for the professions – mainly the 'learned' ones, the clergy, medicine and law – but recruitment was personal, through apprenticeship and through family and local networks. The change came when professionalisation required objective and nationally valid tests, membership of defined professional bodies, and an extended theoretical training.

The reform of the Scottish universities was powered ultimately by the desire of the Scottish middle class to retain its position in this more competitive world, but the reform process was supervised by the state, being one of the many successful and sometimes ruthless Victorian adaptations of old institutions to new needs. Two royal commissions, appointed in 1826 and 1876, drew up reform plans which were, to a large extent, embodied in the Universities (Scotland) Acts of 1858 and 1889.

Each of these acts created a temporary 'executive' commission which imposed detailed prescriptions on each university, in a way which encouraged Scottish uniformity and minimised local variations. Although the need to prepare students for a wide labour market inevitably involved some 'anglicisation', the universities remained a strong element in the Scottish sense of national identity.

While much of the history of reform was common to all the universities, Edinburgh university's relations with the town council were a unique problem. The 1826 commission was appointed partly because of the fraught relations between the two bodies, and it recommended taking the university away from municipal control. But after an abortive attempt to introduce legislation in 1836, nothing was done until 1858. The council retained both detailed control of the university's affairs, including the medical curriculum, the most common flashpoint of conflict with the professors acting as the Senatus, and the university 'patronage' – that is, appointments to chairs. This situation was increasingly at odds with contemporary views on universities, which held that on the one hand they ought to enjoy autonomy in academic affairs, but on the other should conform to national norms, and be responsive to a wider public opinion rather than subjected to the whims of local political, religious and kinship interests. In D. B. Horn's words, the 1826 commission's report in 1831 'foreshadows clearly the later developments which made the universities state agencies, charged with responsibility to Parliament, and bound to play the part assigned to them in what was slowly and painfully becoming a national system of education'.

Following the Reform Act of 1832, Scottish burghs were reformed in 1833. The old oligarchic council was replaced by an elected one, albeit on a narrow property-based franchise. In 1835, a royal commission on municipal corporations underlined the defects of the old, inward-looking system. They pointed out that no Englishman had ever been appointed to an Edinburgh chair, and criticised this 'hereditary holding of office'. In fact, of the twenty-eight professors in office in 1830, all were born in Scotland, and twelve in Edinburgh. Eight were the sons of professors, six of ministers, and most of the others came from the landed or merchant elite. The medical faculty was the most exclusive: of the ten professors, eight were born in Edinburgh, and seven were the sons of professors. This was to change after municipal reform. Formerly tied into the government system of patronage and political management, the council now represented that section of the middle class most concerned with professional education; it was also, according to its critics, over influenced by doctors, some themselves elected as councillors, who abused their position to pursue their own agendas of medical reform. Because of the presence in Edinburgh of the Royal Colleges of Physicians and Surgeons, which had their own rights to grant medical qualifications, and of the voluntarily managed Royal Infirmary, access to whose wards was essential for clinical teaching, the politics of medical education were always complex and often bitter. There was a characteristic conflict in 1855 when an English physician, Thomas Laycock, was appointed to the most prestigious of the medical chairs instead of the favoured internal candidate. This opening up of appointments meant that by 1858, when there were thirty-one professors, eight or nine were born outside Scotland, and only two were sons of professors. The town council thought the prosperity of the university was important to the city's cultural and economic life, saw itself as the organ of enlightened public opinion, and did not appoint men without convincing academic qualifications. But at a time when religious controversy was both acute and closely connected with party politics, the allegiances of candidates were closely scrutinised, and the very public processes of publishing written testimonials, canvassing, lobbying and campaigning in the press were often thought unseemly.

The architecture of the new college – completed by 1832, apart from the dome, which was added in the 1880s – illustrates the contemporary conception of university education. The architects Robert Adam and William Playfair had sought to put everything which a university needed in one building. The only non-clinical teaching off the site was at the Botanic Garden in Inverleith Row, not itself part of the university, where the Professor of Botany gave his lectures; generations of medical students tramped down there in the early morning. The college itself included a library, and a museum to illustrate the teaching of natural history. But otherwise the academic accommodation consisted essentially of large lecture theatres ingeniously packed into the available space. They included an anatomy theatre, to which bodies were discreetly conveyed by a tunnel on the north side of the building. There was provision for apparatus to demonstrate science lectures, but only one small laboratory, for chemistry. When professors began to need laboratories for their own research, or to train advanced students, they had to find makeshift space in cellars or attics. Thus the building was inadequate almost as soon as it was completed, and new needs had to be met by improvisation and adaptation, then by seeking new sites. The opening of the Music School in 1858, following the creation of a music chair in 1839 with the bequest of General Reid, was a pointer to future expansion southwards.

Professors had small 'retiring rooms' adjoining their lecture rooms, but otherwise there were no social or catering facilities for either professors or students. They came in for lectures, then went home again. The professors were few enough to function as a community, and often a quarrelsome one, in which disputes on policy coincided with personal enmities. They did at least get together for an annual dinner. However, to the students, the university offered no collective life, nor did it claim powers of discipline outside its walls. Edinburgh was the most urban and impersonal of the Scottish universities. The daily routine of the student centred around lectures – there were five a week in each course – and was more intense for medical students, who had a more structured curriculum than others, along with clinical instruction in the wards of the Infirmary. But all students lived at home, with relatives or family friends, or in lodgings, the practice of the professors themselves taking boarders having now died out.

A medical student of the 1820s was James Barry, who had a distinguished career in the army medical service. Only after his death was he discovered to be a woman. She thus probably counts as Edinburgh's first female student. (Edinburgh University Library, Special Collections)

Since lecturing had replaced regenting in the eighteenth century, the curriculum was open and flexible. Each professor collected his own fees, usually three guineas a year. Students paid these in cash at the beginning of the year, and at the end of the course were entitled to a class certificate. Candidates for the church – still a large proportion of students, many of whom held bursaries founded over the years to encourage clerical recruitment – had to show attendance at all the main arts courses before entering the divinity faculty. There was an accepted order, extending over four years, in which these should be taken. The curriculum began with Latin (known as humanity), Greek, and mathematics, each of which was taught at two levels. Logic and rhetoric (later renamed English literature) formed the next stage, and moral philosophy and natural philosophy (mathematically based physics) completed the tally of seven subjects.

This curriculum still bore strong traces of what had once been a common European pattern: the faculty of arts gave a preparatory education for the three professional faculties of medicine, law and divinity, and the arts curriculum progressed

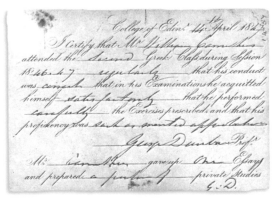

Class certificate issued by George Dunbar, Professor of Greek (1846–7). Once the course was complete, the certificate was endorsed on the back. (University of Edinburgh)

from two years of classical and mathematical study to two years of philosophy. The trend in many countries was to transfer the first year or two of this programme back into secondary schools, and to have a school-leaving examination such as the German *Abitur*, taken around the age of eighteen and acting as the test for university entry. This required high-level secondary schools throughout the country, and these did not yet exist in Scotland; Edinburgh Academy, opened in 1824, provided a model, but was an expensive private school confined to the social elite. Thus, Scottish university students could still arrive at the age of fifteen or sixteen (sometimes younger) and begin their studies in the first-year 'junior' classes in Latin, Greek and mathematics. Only a basic knowledge of Latin was needed, and this could be picked up in parish schools, where the masters were expected to be university men. The parish-school system was unique to Scotland, and was prized by public opinion for keeping the channels of mobility open to boys from modest social backgrounds and remote rural areas – the famous 'lads o' pairts', though that term was not yet in use. Reformers, however, starting with the 1826 commission, argued that there should be a clear separation between secondary and university education and a higher age of entry, with scholarships at school level for the talented boys who had formerly come through the parish schools, an entrance examination to exclude ill-prepared students, and a shift from elementary survey work to a more complex curriculum giving opportunities for specialisation. The struggle between those who wished to move to this continental pattern and defenders of the tradition of open and 'popular' university education was resolved only in the 1890s.

One professor, asked by the 1826 commission about the possibility of a final examination with 'a classification, according to merit or proficiency', replied that 'the subject is rather new to me, the proceeding is so utterly unknown in this University'. Students who wanted to distinguish themselves could compete for class prizes, but otherwise did no more than accumulate class certificates. Formal graduation in arts had become rare; it involved extra fees, and in the 1830s there were only half a dozen graduations a year. Moreover, there were numerous students who did not go through the full curriculum, but only picked what lectures they needed, and the system gave much scope for part-time and short-term study. Most law students were part-timers, working in offices during the day, while students from poorer backgrounds might combine study with schoolteaching. Further up the social spectrum, the local gentry and the merchant elite often sent their sons for a year or two of classics and philosophy to polish off their general education. The urban character of the university encouraged these habits, and led the Edinburgh Senatus to oppose the royal commission's plans for an entrance examination and tighter curriculum requirements. Curricular freedom, it claimed, was the secret of the university's constant adaptation to new needs, as well as holding the door open to 'the studious youth, whose means, both pecuniary and educational, are limited'.

While medical and law students generally selected a few arts courses without prolonging their preparatory studies, conversely 'arts' students in search of a broad and useful education could take the science courses which had developed as part of the medical faculty – botany, chemistry and natural history (which then combined geology and zoology). Although the natural sciences were not part of the traditional arts sequence, they had a particular interest at this time: chemistry because of its successful applications to industry and agriculture, natural history because the mounting intellectual controversies over the age of the earth and the evolution of species put them at the cutting edge of religious controversy. The idea of 'natural theology' – that nature displayed the power and benevolence of the Creator – was not an easy one to abandon. Given the influence of the rural clergy on economic improvement, the church itself favoured some science education for its ministers, and many other members of the elite took from their university years an abiding interest in the natural world. Thomas Hope's huge Chemistry classes, angled to the general public, were exceptional, but other science professors of this period, like Robert Jameson in natural history and Robert Graham and John Hutton Balfour in botany, conducted classes of 200 or more, supported by classroom demonstrations and collections of material built up at their own expense. New chairs could also find a niche if they met the needs of a particular group of students. Agriculture (founded in 1790) was able to do this, while civil history (1719) and astronomy (1786) did not. The history chair came to be regarded as 'a subsidiary and temporary appointment for advocates of a literary turn'; Cosmo Innes (1846–74) was an able historian, but soon gave up lecturing as he was unable to attract a class. The first Professor of Astronomy, Robert Blair, filled the post for forty-two years, but was rarely seen in Edinburgh. This was perhaps understandable as he was given no observatory, but even when the state provided one in the 1830s, and combined the chair with the post of Astronomer Royal for Scotland, Blair's successors did no teaching.

In the 1830s classes in the standard arts subjects usually numbered between 150 and 200. The lecture was the central form of teaching, though in some subjects the professors also put questions to the class and corrected written essays. Some professors ran informal classes for advanced students. William Hamilton, Professor of Logic, a teacher who made a strong personal impression on his pupils, did this in the 1830s, and his

pupil and successor Alexander Campbell Fraser followed suit in
the 1860s. These were the ancestors of the modern Honours
class. But it was only in the 1830s and 1840s, as part of a general
tightening up of the course requirements in arts, that students
were introduced to that nineteenth-century invention destined
to tyrannise British education, the written examination. The
aim of the Senatus was to encourage graduation, and in 1842
it introduced a BA degree with lower requirements than the
MA, which could be completed in three years. Even so, by the
1860s only about a dozen students a year took the MA, and
rather fewer the BA.

In medicine, on the other hand, graduation was important
because it gave the right to practise. Here, too, the regulations
were progressively made stricter, and four years of study were
normally required. At this time, the dominant idea in medical
education was the centrality of clinical observation, though this
did not generally mean direct contact between students and
patients, but demonstration lectures by the professors, tracking
down disease by diagnosis of the living patient in the hospital
ward and dissection of the dead one on the mortuary slab. The
new science of pathology acquired a chair at Edinburgh in

Allen Thomson, Professor of Institutes of Medicine (Physiology) (1842–8). He was noted for work in microscopic anatomy, and is photographed with his microscope. (Edinburgh University Library, Special Collections)

Cartoon of a medical class, 1855. (University of Edinburgh)

1831. But at Edinburgh the medical professors had rivals in the shape of independent 'extra-mural' lecturers whose classes could also count towards a degree. The most notorious of these was Robert Knox, a lecturer in anatomy, who was supplied with bodies in the 1820s by Burke and Hare. Generally the level of ability of these lecturers was high: they kept the professors on their toes, constituted a pool of ability for filling chairs, and incubated many advances in medical science. Their rights were one of the points of dispute between the university and the town council, but were finally confirmed by a lawsuit in 1854.

Around 1830 the university was at a numerical peak. Student statistics for this period are difficult to interpret because they were usually only collected for individual classes, and there were many casual attenders. But it was estimated that in 1825 there were 2,144 students: 823 in arts, 892 in medicine, 298 in law, and 131 in divinity. This made Edinburgh one of the largest universities in Europe. But in subsequent years numbers declined sharply, whether because of the university's quarrels with the city, or because of wider fluctuations in the demand for professional men. The number of matriculated students fell steadily, to 1,056 in 1844 (and in medicine to 370). Lord Cockburn, the Whig judge and commentator on his times, attributed this to the disappearance of the more famous professors ('the old lights are gone'), and to the obsolescence of traditional university culture ('the old half-superstitious reverence for colleges is greatly worn out'). Other factors included the development of hospital-based medical schools in London and other English towns, and in the 1840s the problems were compounded by the Disruption.

The Disruption was the crisis in the Scottish established church over the relations of church and state, which led to a large breakaway of ministers and congregations to form the Free Church. Although there were no religious tests for students in the Scottish universities, professors were required to subscribe to the Church of Scotland's doctrinal statement, the Westminster Confession. At Edinburgh, this was only loosely

Thomas Chalmers.
(Edinburgh University
Library, Special
Collections)

enforced: the Professor of Mathematics in 1838–79, Philip
Kelland, was an Anglican clergyman. But the Disruption forced
divinity professors who joined the Free Church to surrender
their chairs, including the charismatic preacher and national
celebrity Thomas Chalmers. The Free Church set up its own
college, New College, to train ministers. This was a severe blow
to the university, whose divinity faculty now had to compete
with rivals, including those of other dissenting Presbyterian
churches. The Disruption also created new tension between
the university and the town council, as the majority of the

latter were Free Churchmen or dissenters, who made some appointments which deliberately challenged the law. This situation lasted until an Act of Parliament of 1853 abolished the test for secular chairs, substituting an innocuous declaration (which was itself abolished in 1889). The abolition of tests made the intrusion of political and denominational factors in town-council appointments seem all the more anomalous.

The 1850s saw a general revival of the cause of university reform, which had two prominent advocates in Edinburgh. One was John Stuart Blackie, who was appointed to the chair of Greek in 1852 and held it for thirty years. He previously held a chair at Aberdeen, where he had already stirred up controversy over the religious test. Blackie became a well-known public figure, took up many causes, and was later notable for his championing of the Highlands and for the campaign which created a chair of Celtic, Scotland's first, in 1882. But in the 1850s, disaffected with the need to teach Greek virtually from scratch, he campaigned above all for the raising of intellectual standards and the relegation of routine teaching to the schools. Blackie had studied at Göttingen and Berlin, and shared this German experience with the second reformer, James Lorimer, an Edinburgh advocate who was to become Professor of Public and International Law in 1862, and who took a high view of the state's responsibility to support science and scholarship and to create new university posts.

Blackie and Lorimer were among the first spokesmen in Britain for the highly influential German, or 'Humboldtian', model of the university (after Wilhelm von Humboldt, who founded the University of Berlin in 1810). This model had two aspects. First, the exaltation of classical education, and especially the study of Greek civilisation, as a unique instrument for the formation of the personality. German 'neo-humanism' attributed a central intellectual role to 'philology', the study of languages and texts, which in Scotland was thought by many to conflict with the traditional emphasis on philosophy and 'metaphysics'. The application of critical philological techniques to the text of the Bible could also have subversive

John Stuart Blackie,
photographed in the
1880s. His plaid and
broad-brimmed hat
were a trademark and
distinguished him at
a time when most
professors wore sober
garb. (Edinburgh
University Library,
Special Collections)

consequences, and when the government created a chair of
biblical criticism in 1846 – one of the few recommendations of
the royal commissioners carried out before 1858 – it was to
strengthen Christian teaching against this threat. Second, the
Berlin model saw the advancement of knowledge, not just its
transmission, as the essential function of the university.
According to the principle of the 'unity of teaching and
research', the professor's prime duty was to advance the fron-
tiers of his subject, while initiating his students into the spirit
of independent research. As the Scottish universities were
strongly oriented towards broad, liberal teaching and commit-

ted to the lecture method, this, too, was controversial.

Lorimer founded an Association for the Improvement and Extension of the Scottish Universities in 1853. University reform returned to the political agenda, with a wave of pamphlets, public meetings, and delegations to London, and Lorimer's political contacts helped bring about the Universities (Scotland) Act of 1858, which disposed of many of the questions left hanging since the 1830s, notably the constitutional ones. But the old debate about raising the entrance age and redefining the boundary between secondary and university education remained open. In addition to the practical arguments about the need to keep the universities open to the parish schools (and the professors' reluctance to lose the large fee income from their first-year classes), a strong body of Scottish opinion held that any restriction on entry was wrong, as the universities were public institutions, which ought to be open to all citizens.

Constitutionally, the 1858 Act took control of the university out of the hands of the town council, though this was resisted to the last by the latter. As a concession, appointments to existing chairs (and to the Principalship) were given to a special body, the Curators of Patronage, with joint municipal and university membership. Otherwise supreme authority was to lie with the University Court, which was designed to balance various interests. It was to be chaired by the Rector, elected by the students (this was a new office in Edinburgh); other members were the Principal, the Lord Provost, and 'assessors' appointed by the Rector, the town council, the Chancellor (a new and mainly ceremonial office), the professors and another new body, the General Council, consisting of all graduates. Day-to-day academic policy and administration remained in the hands of the Senatus, consisting of all the professors. In 1889, there was a shift of authority towards the Court, whose membership was enlarged, and which took over financial responsibility from the Senatus. With later modifications, this structure has survived. The 1889 Act also ensured that the 'patronage' of new chairs, usually retained by the crown in the

past, would lie with the Court. But this was slow to take effect: by 1900 the Court appointed directly to only four chairs, the other appointments being shared between the Curators, the crown, and various mixed bodies, in which the Edinburgh legal profession predominated. If control of its own membership is a mark of university autonomy, Edinburgh University still had significant accountability to outside interests.

The Principal chaired the Senatus, and in the absence of the Rector and Chancellor (which was normally the case) the Court and General Council as well. The office was thus a pivotal one. All recent principals were clergymen, and saw their role as pastoral as well as administrative. John Lee, who had been Principal since 1840, combining the post with a divinity chair, died in 1859. The town council, acting for the last time before the 1858 Act took effect, appointed the scientist David Brewster. Now aged seventy-eight, and noted for his discoveries in optics, he was the main founder of the British Association and a public champion of science and technology. However, the appointment also had a political aspect. Brewster was a Free Church layman, and the established church had tried to get him dismissed from his previous post at St Andrews. While celebrating the achievements of modern industry, Brewster also held to a traditional 'natural theology' standpoint. In his first address to the students in 1859 (the year of Darwin's *Origin of Species*), he claimed that 'the instruction of literary and theological students, and indeed of the whole population, in the grand truths of the material world' was 'the duty of a Christian Church and a Christian State'.

Brewster also observed that the 1858 Act had given the university 'corporate independence', and it was indeed a landmark both in the secularisation of education and in redefining the relationship between the university and the state. The university was now largely free both from religious obligations (apart from the divinity faculty) and from the play of local politics and interests. As the Act itself showed, universities in Scotland were seen indisputably as public institutions, and the state had always contributed to their costs, mainly through fixed salaries paid to the professors. These were now increased, and the state also paid for assistants in some of the more hard-pressed chairs. Of an additional £10,000 a year for the Scottish universities, Edinburgh got £3,345. But in return the universities were regulated by detailed 'Ordinances', drawn up by a temporary commission, and only changeable thereafter with the consent of the privy council, to which the other three universities might object. For in both constitutional and curricular matters, one aim of the 1858 and 1889 Acts was to preserve national uniformity.

The university's annual income from the state after 1858 amounted to about £7,800. But apart from £575 given as compensation for the Library's loss of copyright privileges, all of this went to pay salaries. The government had helped with the completion of the Old College, and proved willing to do so again when a new medical school was built. But there was no general provision for capital expenditure or for financing new developments. Not for the last time, therefore, a campaign was launched to appeal to graduates and wealthy individuals. An Edinburgh University Club was founded in London in 1864, and in the same year an Association for the Better Endowment of the University of Edinburgh was set up to make the university's needs known and encourage individual benefactors. Benefactions began to flow in, though donors or testators preferred to attach their names to bursaries or prizes, which helped individual students rather than the university's general revenues. Richer donors might found chairs in new subjects, which were welcome, and which were supplemented in most cases by an extra state grant, but their enthusiasms did not necessarily reflect immediate teaching priorities.

The 1858 executive commission, headed by John Inglis, who had carried the Act through as Lord Advocate, was composed of lawyers, aristocrats, and MPs, without any academic members. In its Ordinances of 1863 on the arts curriculum, which derived ultimately from the proposals of the 1826 royal commission, it reflected a decidedly professional ideal of liberal education. Graduation was to be encouraged (it conferred membership of the General Council, and from 1868 to 1948 a university vote in general elections), but the MA programme was to be a uniform and rigorous one based on the traditional seven subjects. Edinburgh's BA degree was abolished. According to the commission's plan, there was to be a balance of classical, philosophical and mathematical subjects. They thought it 'superfluous to enlarge' on the benefits of Latin and Greek, while also praising the long and distinguished Scottish metaphysical tradition, with its 'special and most beneficial influence on the national character'.

However, it was characteristic of that tradition that training the mind through observation and experiment was not included in the scheme, and it was left to individual universities whether they chose to add a natural science to the standard

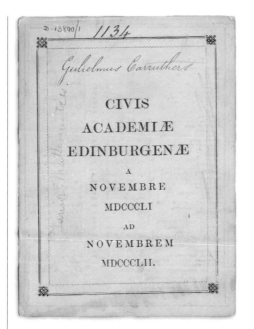

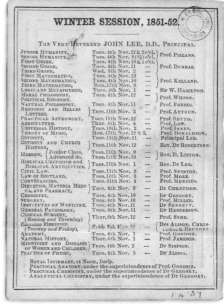

curriculum. Aberdeen and St Andrews did, but Edinburgh did not, despite repeated complaints in the General Council. On the other hand, Greek remained compulsory, which was both academically conservative and socially elitist, as Greek teaching in schools was limited. In practice, the danger of social exclusion was avoided, as an entrance examination was still firmly rejected, and the first-year junior classes were retained, though better-qualified students were now allowed to miss them out and take their degree in three years. It also became possible to take an Honours degree, in one of four groups: classics, mathematics, philosophy and natural science. This introduced to Scotland the classified degree and the Oxbridge cult of examination performance. Those aiming at Honours had to complete the full standard curriculum first, and usually stayed on for a short while to work for the extra examinations, but there were still no systematic Honours classes. As most subjects were studied for just one year, the possibilities for specialisation were very limited. The idea that there should be a single form of liberal education to mould all university men was still a very powerful one, tied up with contemporary ideas of 'gentlemanly' status; just a few years before, John Henry Newman had given the series of lectures at Dublin embodying this ideal, which were later published as *The Idea of a University*.

The commission's Ordinances also covered medical education, coinciding with a landmark in the history of professionalisation, the Medical Act of 1858. This made medical education uniform throughout the United Kingdom, and effectively prevented anyone who was not a medical graduate from practising as a doctor. At Edinburgh, the result was a thoroughly revised four-year curriculum, though there was no money for new chairs. The scientific side of the subject was strengthened in various ways; the full integration of medicine and surgery was especially significant, and was marked by the joint title of the standard degree the MB, CM (Bachelor of Medicine, Master of Surgery). But before entering on the medical curriculum, students had to pass a preliminary examination in arts subjects, including compulsory Latin; many students thus needed to spend a preparatory year or two in the arts faculty. The 1858 reforms confirmed the parallel rights of the Royal Colleges to grant qualifications, and of the extra-mural lecturers to give courses that counted for the university degree.

The commissioners also sought to strengthen professional training in law and theology, where degree examinations and formal graduation had been unknown. In theology, denominational sensitivities prevented the commission creating a bachelor's degree, though the university introduced its own in 1864. But in law, they created a LL.B degree, open only to arts graduates. It was meant to encourage the academic study of law, and the commission followed this up by turning the sinecure chair of civil history into a chair of constitutional law and history, and by reviving the vacant chair of public law, which was given to Lorimer. Lorimer believed that law should be a scholarly and liberal study, not just a training for practitioners, and he argued that an expanded legal education could give a broad preparation, as in continental countries, for public service, diplomacy, journalism and similar careers. But this idea never caught on in Britain. The LL.B proved too advanced to attract more than a handful of candidates, nor did a less demanding BL

degree created by the university in 1874 have any more success. What mattered was acceptance into the professional bodies: it had been a sign of rising standards when the Faculty of Advocates insisted on an arts degree in 1854, but this was not expected of most law students, who took only the basic classes in Scots law and conveyancing, often while already working as apprentices, and even this was not compulsory until the Law Agents Act of 1873.

While Brewster celebrated corporate independence, there

were others who drew on the history of European universities to claim that by the 1858 Act the university was 'transformed into a self-governed society of graduates, and reconstituted on this foundation'. If the local professional elites had lost the chance of influencing the university through the town council, they could now do so through the General Council. From the 1860s to the 1890s, local graduates used it to campaign vigorously on a number of issues, which often brought them into conflict with the professoriate, who were accused of blocking change because of the fees which they drew from the compulsory subjects. Since professors themselves were members of the Council, its meetings could be exploited against their colleagues by professors who championed curricular reform such as David Masson (English literature) and the irrepressible Blackie. The Council also campaigned for an extension of its own powers, and General Council agitation, in all four Scottish universities, was one reason for the appointment of a new royal commission in 1876.

This commission included two of the leading national spokesmen for science, Thomas Huxley and Lyon Playfair. Both had Edinburgh connections. Huxley was currently standing in for Wyville Thomson, Professor of Natural History, while he was cruising the world on HMS *Challenger* in a famous oceanographic expedition. Playfair had been Professor of Chemistry before becoming one of the first Scottish university MPs in 1868, and was noted for his advocacy of scientific and technical education as essential to national prosperity, and for the view that universities should expand into training new and evolving professions as well as the old 'learned' ones. The report of the royal commission suggested a radical overhaul of the whole curriculum, with a new emphasis on science and far more specialisation.

This was rejected at the time, yet the new arts curriculum had proved controversial from the start for its lack of flexibility and its neglect of science. The absence of the natural sciences in the standard curriculum meant that few students took Honours in the subject. In 1864, the university decided to

A group thought to be
Wyville Thomson with
his students or assis-
tants. He was Professor
of Natural History
(1870–82). (Edinburgh
University Library,
Special Collections)

Fleeming Jenkin, first
Professor of
Engineering (1868–85).
The 1884 engraving
shows his invention
of 'telpherage', an
electrically powered
overhead conveyor
system. (Edinburgh
University Library,
Special Collections)

bypass the 1858 system altogether by creating a BSc degree, which could be embarked on without Latin, and required a grounding in all the science classes before specialising at the final stage. This flexible degree was used to incorporate new subjects such as public health and agriculture, and to assimilate the creation of new chairs. A chair of engineering was endowed in 1868 by the Dundee industrialist Sir David Baxter, and a chair of geology was financed personally in 1871 by the Scottish geologist Roderick Murchison, allowing the Professor of Natural History to concentrate on zoology. In the 1870s, because of their dual medical and general role, classes like natural history and chemistry were among the largest in the university.

As long as the MA degree lacked this flexibility, new subjects for which there was a clear demand, or for which donors were willing to pay, could not be fitted in. The first endowed chair founded after 1858, and the first new arts chair since 1760, was in Sanskrit (1862). The founder was John Muir, a retired Indian civil servant and scholar, who was also a leading figure in the Endowment Association. The chair reflected the interest of graduates in the new Indian Civil Service examinations, and Sanskrit was a prestigious subject at the time because of philological interest in the roots of the classical and oriental languages. There followed a chair of political economy, endowed in 1871 by the Merchant Company, a wealthy corporate body representing the Edinburgh business community. Like engineering, this subject attracted a specific part-time clientele of young men working in offices, but economics could not develop its wider potential until it could become a graduating subject. The same was true of the Watson Gordon chair of fine art (1879), one of the first university chairs in the subject in Britain, and the chair of Celtic, for which a public appeal orchestrated by Blackie raised £14,000.

Then there was the chair of education, founded in 1876 by the trustees of Andrew Bell, pioneer of the 'Madras' system of elementary education (Madras College at St Andrews was another of his benefactions). This ran into another set of diffi-

culties. The training of elementary teachers was in the hands of
the Scotch Education Department (SED) as it was then called.
Both the established and Free churches had training colleges in
Edinburgh. Men from these colleges often attended individual
arts or science courses to improve their general education, but
they could rarely afford to stay long enough for a degree. The
SED was hostile to universities having any role in professional
training, and it was not yet thought necessary for secondary
teachers to have any special training beyond an Honours

degree. Thus the distinguished educationist Simon Laurie, who held the chair from 1876 to 1903, never found a real function.

The growth of more systematic secondary education was one of the most important developments of the 1870s and 1880s. From 1885, under the direction of its powerful secretary Henry Craik, the SED encouraged the development of modern secondary schools throughout Scotland, and while the parish-school tradition was becoming obsolete, new opportunities arose for rural children to attend schools in nearby towns. In Edinburgh itself, large new day schools – George Watson's, Daniel Stewart's, George Heriot's – were created by reforming the endowed 'hospitals', which had been residential institutions for fatherless children. The Edinburgh School Board, created like the SED by the Education Act of 1872, took over the High School from the town council, and also began to develop advanced education in some of its elementary schools (though to a lesser extent than in Glasgow and other towns). All these schools required graduate teachers, yet the university did not teach such basic school subjects as history, geography or modern languages. Nor, of course, did it admit women, at a time when the vigorous development of girls' schools was creating a parallel demand for women graduates. Thus if the university was to serve new needs, and to make proper use of the endowments which it was attracting, a revision of the rigid curriculum devised in 1863 was essential.

The progress of secondary education created the conditions for completion of the nineteenth-century reform programme. In the 1860s, there was a very wide range of ages on entry, but most students who came direct from school did so between fifteen and seventeen. By 1890 the age-range had narrowed, as secondary schooling became the norm, and entry was typically at seventeen or eighteen. In 1888, the SED created a broad-based Leaving Certificate (the ancestor of Highers) usually taken at seventeen, and it was a small step from this to a university entrance examination. At the same time, efforts within the university to encourage graduation were bearing fruit. In 1859, only eighty-seven students graduated, of whom sixty-two were medical. In 1890–1, there were ninety-eight MAs, including seventeen with Honours, and thirty-six BSc's alongside 250 taking the medical degree. Seventeen students took the Bachelor of Divinity degree, and nineteen the LL.B or BL. Graduation was not yet universal, but it was becoming the norm.

The Universities Act of 1889, which followed a prolonged period of legislative gestation in the 1880s, tidied up various constitutional and financial matters, admitted women to the Scottish universities, and arrived at what proved a longstanding compromise on the curricular question. Most of these changes were introduced by Ordinances in 1892. There was to be a compulsory Preliminary Examination for entrants, which included one classical language as well as English and mathematics. Most Scottish students used the Leaving Certificate as the equivalent. The junior classes were abolished, and students now began at what had been second-year level. Thus an Ordinary degree (as it was now called) could be completed in three years. The uniform degree was abolished, but choice was constrained by a system of subject groups, and every curriculum had to contain a classical language, English or a modern language, logic or moral philosophy, and mathematics or natural philosophy. The Honours degree was now separated clearly from the Ordinary degree, and involved study of selected subjects at an advanced level, adding a fourth year of study; but for the first two years the curricula were not differentiated, as Honours students had to take subjects from three groups as well as the group in which they took Honours. This structure allowed recently developed subjects to be slotted in, and new ones to be introduced: the commissioners created a chair in history and lectureships in modern languages. The changes brought Scotland into line with the continental pattern of relations between schools and universities, broadened the concept of the 'democratic intellect' by extending it to women and by abolishing compulsory Greek, and gave full academic citizenship to modern subjects. The fact that degrees could now be completed in three years made them more accessible to the working-class students coming up through the new urban secondary schools, and for such students teaching had replaced the church as the classic path of social mobility.

How far did the reforms since 1858 change the nature of the student body? An official survey of the 1860s tells us the fathers' occupations of two samples of arts students. Roughly 35 per cent came from professional families (such as ministers, doctors and lawyers), 15 per cent from the richer business class, and 15 per cent from farming. But about 8 percent were drawn from shopkeeping or white-collar families, and 25 per cent from the working-class – though most of the 'working class' fathers were skilled craftsmen rather than labourers, miners or factory workers. These figures show that, as one might expect, the student body was predominantly middle class, yet also that in Scotland the relatively low fees and living expenses, and the availability of many charitable bursaries, put a university educa-tion, and thus entrance into the professions, within reach of a wide social range. An open, urban university like Edinburgh had a very different profile from Oxford and Cambridge. It was also open to older men in their twenties or thirties, often from poorer backgrounds, who had saved enough money to pay their fees. These mature students, along with casual attenders, tended to be squeezed out as the university acquired a more homogeneous clientele coming straight from school and aiming at graduation. The fathers' occupations of students after the 1860s are not known, but there may well have been some decline in the proportion coming from the working class. In the 1900s, however, the Carnegie Trust founded by the Scottish-American millionaire Andrew Carnegie began to pay the university fees of Scottish-born students. In 1912 about two-thirds of the arts students were beneficiaries, and of those a third had fathers in 'manual occupations', equivalent to some 20 per cent overall.

We also have evidence of students' geographical origins, showing that Edinburgh was always the most cosmopolitan of the Scottish universities. Its medical reputation particularly attracted outsiders. Between the 1870s and the First World War, with relatively little fluctuation, 65–70 per cent of students were born in Scotland, predominantly in the Lothians and other parts of eastern Scotland. The proportion coming from the rest of the United Kingdom was about 20 per cent initially, but fell to 11 per cent by 1910, while overseas students rose from 14 per cent in the 1880s to 20 per cent in 1910, mostly from the British Empire. Students from the white dominions, many from families with Scottish origins, were prominent in student life from the late nineteenth to the mid–twentieth centuries. But missionary links also brought black students from western and southern Africa at quite an early stage, and by the 1870s the Indian government was sending a regular contingent of students. In 1933, a survey of Edinburgh's 19,501 graduates showed that only 10,782 were living in Scotland, 5,405 of them in Edinburgh and Midlothian; 5,422 were in other parts of the British Isles, and 3,297 overseas, the largest groups being in South Africa (769) and India (751), with 573 in Australia and New Zealand, 216 in the United States, 174 in Canada, and 134 in China. Scotland was unable to absorb all the graduates which its universities produced, and while most of Edinburgh's students had strong local roots, the function of a university education was often to uproot them. The reforms of the nineteenth century allowed the university both to adapt successfully to the new demand for professional qualifications tested by examination, and to feed its graduates into careers in Scotland, in Britain, and in the British Empire.

CHAPTER 2

The Growth of Corporate Life

In 1884 the university celebrated its 300th anniversary with an elaborate set of events designed to mark both the university's prosperity and its place in the international community of universities. This appears to have been the first British event of the kind, though such jubilees were common on the continent. Delegates were invited from every university in the world, and the high point was the award of honorary degrees to 121 distinguished men. Amid the throng of celebrities, the greatest catches were the Frenchman Louis Pasteur and the German Rudolf Virchow, scientists famous for their contributions to medicine and public health. There were numerous other events spread over four days, including a town council reception for 4,000 guests and a banquet where over a thousand sampled 'haggis à l'écossaise' among the seven courses. This started at 6.30 p.m., and overran until 12.30 a.m., so effusive were the toasts and replies, testing the patience even of a Victorian audience inured to long sermons and Gladstonian speeches. The official celebrations ended with a firework display on the Castle Esplanade. Attractions laid on for those making a holiday of it included 'an invitation to witness a football match at Tynecastle, one of the western suburbs of Edinburgh', which probably enlarged the visitors' English vocabulary.

These ceremonies were masterminded by Sir Alexander Grant, Brewster's successor as Principal. Grant inherited a Scottish baronetcy, but had not grown up in Scotland. A product of Harrow and Balliol College, where he was a pupil of Benjamin Jowett, he was one of a number of academics at this time who brought the Oxford ideal of classical 'Greats' to Scotland. An expert on Aristotle, he had given up a scholarly career to become an educational administrator in India before coming to Edinburgh. He had strong views on university autonomy, which he expressed in a two-volume history of the university written for the tercentenary. These exertions were probably responsible for Grant's early death later in 1884. He was succeeded by Sir William Muir, another retired Indian administrator, who steered the university through the legislative upheavals of 1889, and who gave way in turn in 1903 to William Turner, the Professor of Anatomy.

Grant's appointment – the first by the Curators of Patronage – had been controversial, as he was the candidate of the professors against the 'town' candidate, the surgeon James Young Simpson. But Grant established cordial relations with the local community, and perhaps his greatest achievement was to raise funds for the new Medical School. The tercentenary, which should really have been held in 1882 or 1883, was delayed to coincide with its opening. Since 1861 (when reliable annual statistics first become available) the total number of students had more than doubled, from 1,462 to 3,423, but medical students had tripled, from 543 in 1861 to 1,736 in 1884. The limitations of the arts degree did not inhibit expansion, as a university education became more valuable for professions of all kinds, but it is the dominance of medicine which is striking in this period. By 1880 over half the student population was in the medical faculty, and this lasted until the 1900s. As a result, overcrowding in Old College became acute. When the Royal Infirmary was rebuilt on a new site, opening in 1879, it made sense for the medical school to follow; the process is being repeated 120 years later. Developments in medical teaching meant that students were now expected not only to have clinical experience, but also to work individually at the laboratory bench. As the new science of bacteriology supplemented pathology and physiology, the microscope became more than ever a tool of medicine. Only a new building could provide the necessary laboratory space. An appeal was launched in 1874 and raised nearly £150,000. Robert Rowand Anderson's original design for the 'New Buildings', in Italian Renaissance style,

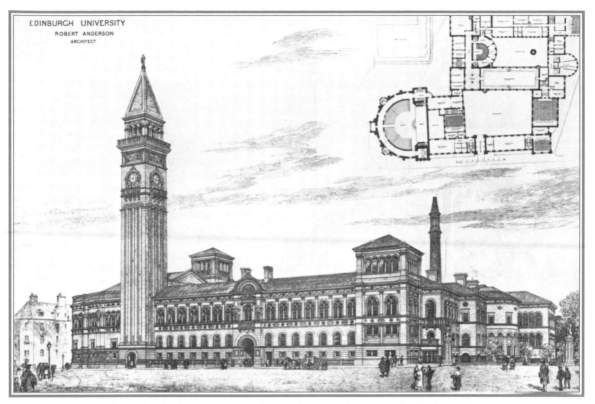

EDINBURGH UNIVERSITY
ROBERT ANDERSON
ARCHITECT

included a campanile and a graduation hall, but these were dropped in order to gain a subsidy of £80,000 from the government.

The graduation hall was to be added in 1897, the brewing millionaire William McEwan meeting most of the cost of £115,000 – a fitting tribute to generations of student consumption. The demand for such a hall was itself significant. When the numbers graduating were small, the 'laureation' ceremonies could be held in a classroom. But reformers like Grant wanted to encourage graduation, and there was a general demand for greater dignity and ceremonial in university affairs, part of a contemporary movement which historians have dubbed the 'invention of tradition'. For the tercentenary ceremony, the university had to borrow the United Presbyterian Synod Hall, but the McEwan Hall gave the university a ceremonial home of its own, complete with an organ and murals by William Palin illustrating the arts and sciences.

Greater ceremonial dignity also meant suppressing the

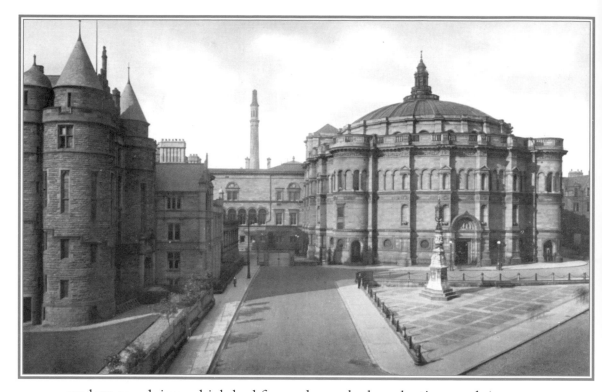

student rowdyism which had formerly marked graduations and other public events. Students sang, drowned the speeches of distinguished visitors with shouts and musical instruments, threw missiles, and let off fireworks. At a time of strict social conventions, there was an element of ritual reversal in these manifestations, as well as the release of juvenile high spirits, but they embarrassed the university authorities. Grant began his Principalship by giving an annual address at the beginning of the session, as Brewster had, but gave it up because of the rowdyism. As the tercentenary approached, the Senatus encouraged a group of students who founded the Students' Representative Council (SRC) to take control of student discipline, and decorum was successfully established. The students organised their own programme of events, including a torch-light procession (a student speciality on festive occasions), a theatre show, a grand ball, and a giant 'symposium', or 'smoking concert'.

The main founder of the SRC was Robert Fitzroy Bell, a senior law student, who is said to have taken the idea from a

The completed McEwan Hall. The Medical School is in the background, and the Students' Union to the left; the Music School can be glimpsed behind it.

visit to the University of Strasbourg (then in Germany). Once established in 1884, the SRC was quickly imitated in the other Scottish universities, and from 1888 there was an annual inter-university conference. The SRC became a recognised representative body, a focus for student organisations, and a way for ambitious students to gain experience of holding office; the Senior President and two other Presidents rotated the burdens, and over the years a substantial committee network grew up, not least the Amusements Committee, which organised social events and entertainments. Under the 1889 Act, the SRCs were given a modest statutory role, no doubt helped by the fact that Fitzroy Bell was secretary to the executive commissioners: the SRCs had the right to make representations on student matters to the Court and the Senatus, and to be consulted by the Rector before he appointed his Court assessor.

The SRC had shown its ability to keep order at the installation of the new Rector, the politician Sir Stafford Northcote, earlier in 1884. Edinburgh had not had a rector before 1858, but the traditions surrounding the office were taken over from the other Scottish universities. The Rector was elected every three years, and candidates were normally national political leaders, Gladstone being the first. The campaigns were organised by Conservative and Liberal political committees, but were not usually linked with wider political issues. The election campaign itself lasted several weeks, and was accompanied by placards, pamphlets, cartoons, attacks on rival headquarters and the kidnapping of leaders. It culminated in the 'Battle of the Standard' on the day of the poll, when the two parties fought in the Old Quad, with bags of peasemeal as the main weapon. The party which captured the enemy's standard then paraded it down Princes Street. Once elected, the Rector visited Edinburgh to give an inaugural address, calculated to appeal to the idealism of youth. But these were often received in a different spirit. The installation of the Conservative politician and scholar Sir William Stirling Maxwell in 1872 was exceptional in the scale if not the general character of its rowdyism. A student recorded in his diary:

I can safely say I did not hear a single word. Tambourines, Jews harps, whistles and many other obscene and undefinable instruments of torture were in great requisition; and as the time wore on, the fury increased and the actors passed from simple noise-making to more decided demonstration. The first indication of this was a shower of peas thrown in the direction of the platform, and from this small spark of a beginning, sprang the great fire of missiles which shortly appeared. Peas were for a time the staple commodity of this trade, but soon enterprising students improved on the traditional projectiles and employed bits of biscuit, slices of orange and the like.

The attempts of professors to restore order only made things worse, and the affair ended with a thousand-strong march from the Music Hall in George Street to the university, and then to demonstrate outside the Lord Provost's shop in St Andrew Square (he was William Law, a wealthy grocer and coffee merchant). After 1884, however, the installations themselves were relatively orderly, though some noisy rituals lasted until the 1950s. Real disorder was confined to the election campaign, when the candidates were safely absent.

One reason for the rowdyism at Stirling Maxwell's speech was that passions were inflamed by the question of the admission of women. This occurred late in Scotland by international standards, being delayed until 1892. The most celebrated aspect of the struggle was the attempt of a group led by Sophia Jex-Blake to enter the medical faculty. They succeeded in matriculating in 1869, but opposition soon appeared, and the women were refused access to most classes in the medical school, the male students proving as hostile as many of the professors. Principal Grant was unsympathetic to the women's cause, and litigation went in favour of the university. Jex-Blake and her colleagues were rebuffed, but she returned to Edinburgh to open an independent School of Medicine for Women in 1886, working for the qualifications given by the Royal Colleges. This school and its associated hospital flourished, and in time

A scene from the
rectorial battle of
1920. (University
of Edinburgh)

its students were able to take university examinations and degrees, but Edinburgh (unlike Glasgow) excluded women from full membership of the medical faculty until the First World War. At a time when the London medical schools remained closed to women, Edinburgh's conservatism lost it the chance to capture a developing market.

A second aspect of the women's movement, with deeper local roots, was connected with the growth of academic secondary schools for girls. In 1865 girls were admitted to the 'local' examinations for school leavers which the university had introduced to provide a stimulus to secondary schools, and small private schools were giving way to large modern ones like the two 'ladies' colleges' founded by the Merchant Company in 1870. In Edinburgh as in other towns, the late 1860s saw the creation of university-level lectures for women. The Edinburgh Ladies' Educational Association (later renamed the Edinburgh Association for the University Education of Women) was founded in 1867 by Mary Crudelius, the wife of a German businessman in Leith, and brought together leading supporters of the women's movement. The lectures organised by the association were given by sympathetic arts and science professors, notably David Masson; they were backed up by

essays and examinations, and from 1872 the university awarded
a Certificate in Arts for successful completion of a range of
courses. The lectures met an untapped need, and regularly
attracted 200–300 students, but most of these were from the
leisured middle class, or older women already working as
teachers and looking for a further qualification. The courses
could only serve local students, and were no substitute for the
full university admission for which the association also
campaigned. By 1884 it was clear that the equal admission of
women would be part of the new universities Act already in
the pipeline, yet the issue was ignored at the tercentenary, apart
from the presence of 'ladies' as guests at the main events.

Once the law had been changed, the number of female
students rose fairly rapidly, though they were concentrated in
the arts faculty. The proportion of women students was 10 per
cent in 1903, and rose to a pre-war peak of 19 per cent in 1911,
but of the 639 women students in 1911, 591 were in arts, only
20 in science, and 11 in music, the only faculty where they
outnumbered men (there were also 17 matriculated in medical
classes). As long as teaching was the only graduate career
widely open to women, there was a ceiling on further expansion. By 1914 there were also one or two women assistants on
the university staff, but it was not until 1966 that Edinburgh

appointed a woman professor, Mary Pickford, in physiology.

Speaking at the smoking concert in 1884, Grant praised the contribution of the 'student element' to the tercentenary: 'formerly they existed like isolated atoms, without any cohesion. Now they are a corporate body.' An emphasis on 'corporate life' lay behind many of the innovations of these years, which crystallised into longlasting social patterns. Corporate champions believed that students should form a distinct community within the city, and this ideal was strengthened by the rise in average age and the presence of many students from England and elsewhere outside Scotland, especially in medicine. One of the first priorities of the SRC was the building of a University Union, which was opened in 1887–8 and extended in the 1900s. The Union was financed by student fundraising, not by the university, and a 'Fancy Fair' in 1886 raised £10,000. The new Union was modelled on a gentlemen's club – a more modest Students' Club on similar lines had existed since 1876. It included a restaurant, a library and a debating hall, which became the focus for many university societies and for dances. Membership was, however, by subscription, and only a minority of students joined, particularly medical students since the Union adjoined the new medical school. A second significant development was the foundation of the magazine *The Student* in 1887, which shortly became the official organ of the SRC. All previous student publications had been very short-lived, and designed to display literary talent as much as to reflect student life. *The Student* provided a permanent focus for corporate life, and from 1895 the SRC also published a useful *Students' Handbook*. But in an urban university like Edinburgh, the invention of tradition and the separation of the student community had natural limits, and persistent attempts to introduce the wearing of gowns were never successful.

For Edinburgh remained an essentially non-residential university. Those who did not live at home generally stayed with landladies, who provided board as well as lodging. Marchmont, developed from around 1880 with large tene-

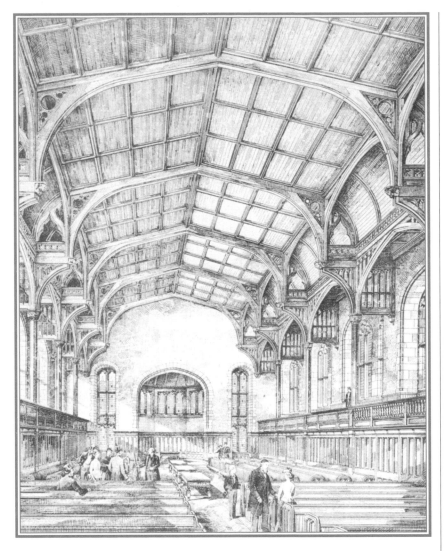

ments well suited to letting, became the classic student area. As
early as the 1860s, there were proposals for student halls, but it
proved impossible to provide accommodation at a rate which
could compete with 'digs'. The main initiative in this area came
from the pioneering social thinker Patrick Geddes, who taught
botany at the university as an assistant. He opened the first of a
series of residences in the Ramsay Gardens area in 1887. These
halls were an experiment in self-government, and were part of
a plan to regenerate Edinburgh's Old Town, but they were relatively expensive for their residents, and remained independent.
After all, around half the students had their homes in

Edinburgh, and had social links based on family and school. In the 1900s, some 40 per cent of students had been educated wholly or partly in Edinburgh. Among men there were particularly large groups from the Academy, the High School, George Watson's, Daniel Stewart's, and Heriot's, while half the women educated in Edinburgh came from the two Merchant Company schools. These backgrounds encouraged cliquishness. But those who came to Edinburgh from outside were also struck by the university's integration into the urban milieu. It was physically situated in a crowded and dingy part of the town, with its own attractions and dangers. 'All the surroundings of the University of Edinburgh have now become hard and business-like, and all sense of academic seclusion and repose is gone,' lamented Grant in 1884. The city provided churches and sports clubs for respectable recreation, taverns and billiard rooms for dissipation. The theatre was the main form of public entertainment (apart from sermons), and well into the twentieth century there were 'student nights' at popular shows, when students filled most of the seats and accompanied the performance with raucous singing and shouting.

For more serious activities, the characteristic organisation was the student society or club. These were active long before the 1880s, and some went back to the eighteenth century like the Royal Medical Society (1737), which had its own premises, and the Speculative Society (1764), which was given its own room in the new college building. These were both elite societies, with membership by invitation. Rather less exclusive were societies like the Dialectic (1787), the Diagnostic (1816, not a medical society despite its name), and the Philomathic (1858), which were general debating societies. Some societies appealed as a rallying-point for compatriots, like the Celtic Society for Highlanders (1848), whose proceedings were partly in Gaelic, and the Dumfriesshire and Galloway Literary Society (1848); there were others for students from the Borders, Caithness and Orkney. Still others were on a subject basis, such as the Theological (1776), the Scots Law (1815), the Philosophical (1871), or the Chemical (1874). Religiously inspired

societies such as the Missionary Association (1825) and the Total Abstinence Society (1853) appealed to others. There were various societies which expressed denominational allegiance or evangelical devotion, and student attitudes generally were still infused by Christian culture and churchgoing habits; there were queues outside popular churches on Sunday mornings, and in the 1900s the Free Church minister John Kelman attracted large audiences to his student sermons at the Operetta House in Chambers Street. But the appearance of an Islamic Society in 1908 and a Jewish Society in 1911, and of the Catholic Chaplaincy in 1912, were symptoms of growing diversity. The overseas students also formed their own clubs: the Indian Association, formed in 1883, was prosperous enough to have its own premises in George Square, and in the 1900s there was a Russian Society 'to promote social relations among students from Russia', many of whom came to western Europe at this time to escape Tsarist restrictions.

In 1833 five of the leading societies (the exact composition varied over the years) grouped themselves into the Associated Societies, and maintained their own hall in Old College. From 1853, when Edinburgh still had no Rector, the Associated

Societies elected a distinguished outsider as an Honorary President who came to deliver an address. Debating was the speciality of these older societies, and they dominated university debating until the 1930s. However, societies of every kind had much the same pattern of activities, alternating between discussion of members' essays and formal debates on a literary, political or ethical question, perhaps followed by a convivial evening of drinking and singing. There might also be an address by a professor at the beginning of the year, a summer outing, and a formal annual dinner, an all-male affair with toasts and musical accompaniment, following a pattern much loved by the Victorian professional classes. Along with alcohol, singing was a significant part of most student occasions, and the *Scottish Students' Song Book*, a joint production of the Scottish SRCs, first appeared in 1891 and was frequently reprinted.

Debating and public speaking were seen as valuable training for public life, and the discussion of essays gave an intellectual stimulus, in a friendly, small-group situation, of a kind otherwise lacking in the Scottish lecture system. The lectures themselves had their own rituals. They dominated the daily routine, and were traditionally accompanied by singing before the professor's entry, whistling, and desk-banging. Some professors played up to this and became popular characters, and when the professor gave the whole lecture course, for five days a week, personalities inevitably made a strong impression. Reminiscences from this period usually give much more space to professors and their classes than to the students' own social lives. Some professors entertained favoured Honours students at home, but most students met them only in the lecture hall; practical classes and tutorials, if they existed, were likely to be conducted by assistants. The reforms of 1892 weakened the impact of the individual professor by multiplying junior staff and abolishing compulsory subjects, and rowdy conduct was modified once women were present, but the old traditions lingered until after 1945. Besides, the development of Honours schools led to an expansion of subject-based societies, as in History (1897), Classics (1898) and German (1899). These were probably the first choice of students without social ambitions, and were open to both men and women.

Academically, women were integrated into the system, attending the same classes as men, though they were expected to come into the lecture hall separately and sit in the front rows. Social integration was more difficult in the years before 1914, when the lives of young middle-class women were hedged around with all kinds of restrictions. Without approved company, they could not easily walk in the city, travel alone, or enter places of entertainment, and formal chaperonage by a married woman was needed at dances and parties. Contact between the sexes was closely monitored, and parents would be reluctant to send their daughters to a university if they thought there was any threat to their respectability. Entering a university where masculine forms of social life were already well established, women had to develop their own social circles. They were barred from joining the Union, and found it difficult to break into student journalism and politics, though the SRC had a Women's Committee elected by the women students. Many societies were open to women, but they also formed their own, including a Women's Debating Society in 1893. Most women students came from the same social backgrounds as men, and lived in digs if their homes were not in Edinburgh. But there was also a demand for halls of residence, and the Association for the University Education of Women devoted its surplus funds to this. Masson Hall was opened in 1897 in George Square, and acted as a social centre for all female students as well as a residence until a Women's Union was opened in 1905. The latter, like the men's Union, was on a subscription basis, but was popular enough to move to larger premises in George Square in 1919.

Another early development now fitted into the corporate pattern was student sport. Games like cricket had been played in Edinburgh in the early nineteenth century, and there were private gymnasia and boxing and fencing classes which had a student clientele. But competitive sport and team games only took off in the 1860s. This reflected the influence of the

Henry Harvey Littlejohn, Professor of Forensic Medicine (1906–27), lecturing with visual aids. He succeeded his father, H. D. Littlejohn, who was Edinburgh's first Medical Officer of Health. Both men were popular lecturers. (Edinburgh University Library, Special Collections)

Sitting-room in the Women's Union, 1913 This was the original Union in Lothian Street. (University of Edinburgh)

C. R. Bauchope, a medical student and noted runner, won four races at the Athletic Club's first Annual Sports in 1866. (Edinburgh University Sports Union)

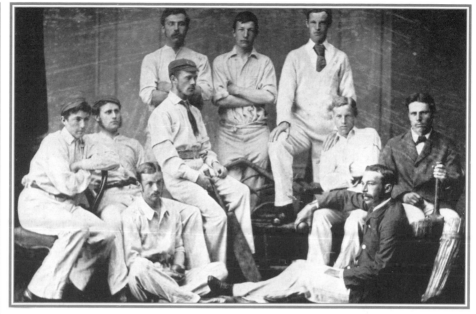

English public schools, but local schools like the Academy (whose sports field dates from 1854), and boarding schools like Merchiston Castle and Loretto, were equally important in the development of sport among middle-class youth. As team games developed in the other Scottish universities, inter-university competitions began to replace matches with local clubs. But Edinburgh students often continued to play for 'former pupils' teams or other city clubs, and this became a perennial complaint in university athletic circles.

A University Athletic Club was formed in 1866, and in the early years field sports were particularly popular. Before the expansion of commercial spectator sports, the annual sports days and inter-university athletics could attract a paying (and gambling) audience from the general public. Later the Athletic Club became a co-ordinating organisation for the individual sports clubs, levying a common subscription, and acting as a channel to the university authorities. The popularity of individual sports came and went, but rugby always had the highest prestige, as it had in the leading Edinburgh schools. University rugby players are recorded in 1857 (in a match against the Academicals), and the club was established by 1871. It was perhaps significant of class and regional differences in sport that

University rugby XV, 1880–1. The velvet cap embroidered with the year, became treasured possessions, and several survive. The bow ties are another elegant touch. (Edinburgh University Library, Special Collections)

the first Association Football club (1877–8) was based not on Edinburgh schools, but on former pupils of Ayr Academy. Like other corporate activities, rugby was especially strong among medical students, and there was a cup for competition between Infirmary ward teams. There were enough 'Australasian' and South African students, no doubt also mostly medics, to have their own sports teams and lively social life. There were also enough Americans and Canadians in the 1890s to support a baseball team.

A medical student and keen sportsman who graduated in 1881 was Arthur Conan Doyle. In Edinburgh he encountered the extra-mural medical lecturer Joseph Bell, who inspired the character of Sherlock Holmes. Holmes never visited Scotland, but medical students and young doctors figure in many of Doyle's other short stories, and his novel *The Firm of Girdlestone* (1890) opens with scenes of Edinburgh student life. His hero is a typically hearty student who throws himself into rugby and the rectorial election, while just scraping through his oral medical exams.

Sport required capital investment in playing fields, and as

Prof. Adam Ferguson, by Sir Henry Raeburn. He was Professor of Moral Philosophy 1764–1816), one of the college's most charismatic professors and a pioneer of social anthropology. (Talbot Rice Gallery, University of Edinburgh)

Prof. John Playfair, by Sir Henry Raeburn. He was Professor of Natural Philosophy (1805–19) and uncle of William Playfair, the second architect of Old College. (Talbot Rice Gallery, University of Edinburgh)

Prof. John Robison, by Sir Henry Raeburn. Professor of Natural Philosophy (1773–1805), Robison was also a noted conspiracy theorist who attributed the causes of the French revolution to a free-masons' conspiracy. (Talbot Rice Gallery, University of Edinburgh)

Robert Adam by James
Tassie. The great
architect was Principal
Robertson's cousin. His
plans for the new
college building were to
be his masterpiece, but
they were too expensive
(Scottish National
Portrait Gallery)

Cricketers at the
opening of the
Craiglockhart
sports field, 1896.
(University of
Edinburgh)

with the Union it was the students themselves who raised most of the money. But the university also contributed, and there was support in higher quarters for activities which developed social skills and employability as well as health. As early as 1855, the Senatus recommended suspending classes on Wednesday afternoons for recreation, though it was not until the 1920s that this was fully observed. The medical professor Robert Christison was an early enthusiast, as was Principal Grant, who had played cricket for Harrow. In the 1870s the university first leased and then bought a field at Corstorphine and built a pavilion there, but this was replaced in 1896 by a ground at Craiglockhart. This cost £12,000, to which the university contributed £2,000, and a bazaar raised a further £3,000 for a pavilion. The increasing official involvement of the university

Cyclists on parade in George Street, 1884. The photo is believed to show the University Cycling Club. (Courtesy of Edinburgh City Libraries)

University volunteers in the 1880s. (University of Edinburgh)

in this aspect of student life was marked by the creation of a permanent Field Committee in 1896. Craiglockhart was a long tram-ride from the university, and sport always suffered because the facilities were not more central. In the 1860s a gymnasium had been fitted up in Old College, but this soon disappeared, and a gym in the new Union suffered the same fate, being converted into a billiard room. Billiards was always a popular recreation, though a questionably athletic one.

In 1902, after the Boer War had revealed the alarming physical state of British youth, a royal commission investigated physical education in Scotland. It found about 350 Edinburgh students taking part in sport – only some 13 per cent of the male student body. Rugby was the most popular section, with seventy-three members; others were Association football, cricket, tennis, hockey, boxing, 'hare and hounds' (cross-country running), golf and rowing. Rowing started in the 1860s, and remained a popular sport at Edinburgh despite the absence of a river: after early outings on a reservoir, the Union Canal at Craiglockhart became its home. In 1902 there was also a beagle pack supported by richer students. Other sports not noted then, but followed at various times, included swimming, water-polo, shinty and cycling. A cycling club flourished in the 1880s, but was devoted to track racing, a popular but short-lived craze, rather than country excursions. Women's athletic clubs also developed, quite separately from the men's. The most popular game was hockey, but the small number of women students and their exclusion from the men's playing fields meant that other sports flourished sporadically. Cycling, tennis, field athletics, rowing, swimming, fencing, and riding were all mentioned at times before 1914, and most of them reappeared after the war, when rowing was especially successful, but only in 1930 did the women gain a permanent sports ground at Peffermill.

As the appointment of the 1902 commission indicates, athleticism could take on patriotic and imperial overtones. A more overtly patriotic activity was military 'volunteering'. This originated in a French war scare in 1859–60, but became an

established popular leisure activity for young middle-class men. The rifle corps was attached to the local regiment, the Royal Scots, and later included a separate Highland company, with the attraction of a kilted uniform. Professors like Christison and Turner acted as officers. There were regular drills in the impressive drill hall in Forrest Road, opened in 1872; with its 29-metre roofspan, it was used for the banquet in 1884. Field days and annual camps, shooting teams and competitions, dinners and other social events made the motives for joining social rather than militaristic. The 1902 commission found that there were 170 students in the infantry, 75 in the artillery battery and 100 in the medical units, which had some vocational value, as the army medical service was a significant outlet for medical graduates. Volunteering was thus far more popular than any single athletic sport. In 1908, university volunteer movements became Officers' Training Corps (OTC), as part of the war minister Richard Haldane's plan to create a reserve of trained officers in case of war. Thus when the call came in August 1914, some 600

The OTC training at North Queensferry, summer 1914. (University of Edinburgh) students and recent graduates were given immediate commissions, and did not return for the new term.

Haldane was elected Rector in 1905. He was the most distinguished Edinburgh graduate in the political world, and known as an expert on university reform. A graduate of the 1870s, he had studied in Germany and become an enthusiast for German philosophy and the German conception of a strong state, retaining a near-professional interest in philosophy while pursuing a successful career at the English bar. His rectorial address in 1907, entitled 'The dedicated life', stressed the ethos of citizenship and service. Universities existed to produce the highest class of national leaders, training them to 'form a part of that priesthood of humanity to whose commands the world will yield obedience'. The university was 'the handmaid of the State of which it is the microcosm – a community in which also there are ruled and rulers, and in which the corporate life is a moulding influence'.

In this exalted concept of the university's mission, the daily round of society meetings, sport and idling in the Union had its own part to play. But whether we look at sport or the OTC, it is clear that only a minority of students took part in the more active forms of corporate life. As officials of the SRC, Union debaters, the editorial committee of *The Student*, the heroes of the rugby club and the OTC, the same names recurred, and there was much cliquishness. Medical students were more active than arts students, as their common life in the laboratories and wards gave them a stronger *esprit de corps* than others. There was a perceptible class barrier as well. The cost of subscriptions, sporting tours, corps uniforms and the formal clothes needed for dinners and dances put an elaborate social life beyond the reach of many poorer students. Like any community of 3,000 people, the student body was a complex organism. The special character of Edinburgh University came from the balance of urban life and corporate feeling, local identity and cosmopolitanism, democratic opportunity and social privilege. That balance was to change only slowly in the twentieth century.

CHAPTER 3

Age of Stability

The changes in the curriculum and student life that had taken place by the 1890s settled into a pattern that lasted until 1939, and in many respects until the 1950s and 1960s, coming in due course to be regarded as 'traditional'. It was a period in which research established itself alongside teaching as a fundamental task, but with the balance still on the side of teaching. The university's relationship with its surrounding community, and with the professions for which it prepared, remained stable. This was reflected in student numbers. In 1885 the university had 3,602 students, and never had as many male students again before 1939; in 1937 there were 4,139 students, of whom 3,132 were male and 1,007 female. In between, the number of male students had dipped as low as 2,559 (in 1900). In other words, growth in student numbers was due mainly to the admission of women.

It was also striking that this stability coincided with a period of population growth: the population of the Lothians grew by 40 per cent between 1881 and 1931. Possibly the professional classes grew more slowly, and expansion was limited by the still very restricted character of secondary education. Even in the 1920s and 1930s, the SED maintained that only a small minority were fitted for university education, and official rhetoric liked to claim that all the appropriate talent was already being discovered and promoted. Probably some 3 per cent of the age group reached higher education, and on the eve of the Second World War, when Edinburgh was admitting about a thousand students a year, only around 4,200 Leaving Certificates were being awarded in the whole of Scotland. Many school leavers went directly into business, where the demand for graduates was still weak. Until family businesses began to give way to

This 'commercial laboratory' in High School Yards was part of the university's development of commercial education. (University of Edinburgh)

corporations with professional managers, that demand came chiefly from organisations like banks, insurance companies and railways. Before 1914 the university resisted calls to develop business education, using existing subjects like economics and modern languages, but after the war, with financial help from local Chambers of Commerce and similar bodies, it created a BCom degree and chairs of accounting (1919) and organisation of industry and commerce (1925).

The BCom degree was relatively successful (20–30 a year in the 1930s), but it was still the professions and public service which were seen as the natural outlet for graduates. The appointments committee set up in the 1900s advised arts and science students how to get into the civil service, various branches of overseas service, and schoolteaching. The most prestigious career, because of its difficult competitive examination, was the civil service, and between 1896 and 1944 there were 222 successful Edinburgh candidates. They were mostly classics or history graduates, and only three held BSc's; equally significantly, 73 of them were ex-pupils of George Watson's College. Edinburgh's contribution to the British governing elite was narrowly based, both socially and intellectually.

Far more graduates became teachers. In 1906, the training of teachers was brought into closer association with the university. The two church colleges in Edinburgh were taken over by the state and merged on the Moray House site, under the rather drab title of Provincial Training Centre. From 1925 the director of the Centre was also the Professor of Education, this being Godfrey Thomson, who stayed until 1951 and was famous for the Moray House psychometric tests, designed to make educational selection fairer and more scientific. The changes in 1906 included new training regulations under which all secondary teachers needed an Honours degree, and prospective primary teachers were encouraged to combine an Ordinary degree with their professional training, taken either concurrently or in a postgraduate year. Later a degree became compulsory for all male teachers. This reform provided a rationale and a clientele for the two types of arts degree introduced in 1892, and by 1910 it was said that over two-thirds of arts students were aiming at teaching.

The entrance examination and the new emphasis on graduation eliminated most casual attenders. The normal stay was now three years – four-year Honours graduates settled down at between a quarter and a third of the total. Lawyers as well as teachers could now graduate before training, and a standard pattern of the Ordinary MA followed by the LL.B flourished in the twentieth century until the advance of specialisation squeezed out a preliminary liberal education for lawyers, as it already had done for doctors. Within the arts degree itself, specialisation remained limited, though some requirements were relaxed in 1908. For the Ordinary degree, subjects now had to be chosen from only three of four groups, none being compulsory (this was partly reversed in 1919 to make one philosophy subject compulsory), and Honours students had to take two instead of three outside subjects. The complexities of the curriculum were eased by the appointment of Official Advisors (later renamed Directors of Studies) to guide students on their choices. But breadth of study remained typical of the Scottish system. This was also true of the three-year BSc degree, now administered by the new Faculty of Science, which had a structure similar to the Ordinary MA, requiring advanced study in three or four subjects. The medical curriculum remained uniform, of course, for all students, and evolved in line with national requirements, but the course was extended from four to five years in 1892, and the first degree renamed MB, ChB.

Another innovation was the introduction of three terms. Before 1908 the 'session' ran from late October to the end of March, with a short break at Christmas; there were just over twenty weeks of teaching, with final examinations and graduation in March and April. This gave students and professors six months of vacation, traditionally justified by the need for the former to earn money in the summer and the latter to recover from the labours of lecturing and to carry out research. But this calendar was widely criticised as wasteful, and over the years a twelve-week 'summer session' had developed between May and July, which was more or less compulsory for medical students, and also used for Honours teaching in arts. However, in 1908 the Scottish universities adopted the English system of three terms running from October to June. At Edinburgh they were called autumn, spring and summer, an ingenious if unconvincing attempt to massage the city's climatic seasons. One purpose of the longer year was to give more space for effective teaching, and to change the balance between lectures and tutorial or laboratory work. Lecturing was cut to three days a week, giving seventy-five lectures in a course instead of a hundred. All were usually still given by the professors themselves, but the reduction in lecturing allowed them to devote more time to Honours teaching, while devolving other tasks to non-professorial staff. But since the number of the latter was still limited, intensive teaching was only really possible in the more advanced classes.

The growth of Honours teaching was linked with the key issue, debated since the 1850s, of the balance between teaching and research. It had always been expected that professors would be appointed for their scientific or scholarly record, and that they would make original contributions to their subjects. But

the systematic pursuit of research as a university priority was a
new idea, with much wider implications. Members of the
science lobby like Huxley and Playfair argued that research was
linked to industrial progress, that universities should develop
subjects relevant to their local industries, and that investment in
science was essential if Britain was to keep up in the competitive international arena. The universities commission of 1876
was only one of several inquiries of the period which took up
this theme. The new ideal also meant the professionalisation of
science and learning. Universities were expected to develop
'postgraduate' work (the term became familiar only in the
1890s), leading to doctorates, and to provide junior posts from

which the next generation of professors could be recruited. Even 'undergraduate' teaching should include an element of the research ethos: in science in the teaching laboratory, in the humanities in the 'seminar', where students examined scholarly problems on the basis of intensive reading. The library, it was often observed, was the laboratory of the arts, and the class library, where Honours students could work amid the necessary sources, became the modest Edinburgh equivalent of the German seminar. Nevertheless, the new approach made slow progress in a system as dominated by written examinations as the Scottish one now was.

The research ideal took time to establish itself. Brewster, for example, believed that scientific research was best pursued in specialised state institutes, that 'successful teaching is the great function which must be performed in our Universities', and that this should be the criterion for appointing professors. But this was already an old-fashioned view, and men with academic ambitions had begun to visit the continent to absorb the new ideas at source. Medical professors had studied in the great hospitals of Paris quite early in the nineteenth century, but it was Germany which became the mecca for academics before 1914, as America was to be later. In 1884, seventeen of the thirty-eight professors had studied in continental Europe, giving substance to the cosmopolitan claims of the tercentenary. But providing the infrastructure for research and research-based teaching posed formidable financial problems, as the building of the medical school showed. In the 1860s, donors began to create scholarships for travel or advanced study, and in 1864, along with the BSc, the university created a DSc degree, which could be taken, despite its name, in arts subjects as well as science. But this was awarded on the results of higher examinations, not research. Real development of postgraduate work came with the 1889 commissioners. The titles of research student and research fellow were introduced, vocational diplomas in scientific and medical subjects began to appear, and the DSc was replaced in 1895 by three separate doctorates (DSc, DPhil and DLitt), which were expected to take five years, and which were based on a research thesis. Like the earlier doctorate, however, these attracted only a handful of candidates – four or five a year in science by 1914, but only one or two a year in arts.

In 1919, in common with other British universities, Edinburgh introduced the rather less challenging PhD, originally devised to attract American students after the war had stripped German universities of their lustre. Although the divinity faculty succeeded in attracting overseas students to the PhD, otherwise few foreigners came, and the degree was taken up by British students. Yet numbers remained small right down to 1939. By then nine or ten PhDs a year were awarded in arts, a dozen in divinity, and around twenty-two in science. In science, research training had vocational value because there were research jobs in government and industry, but in arts there was little of what would today be called a 'research culture', and even less in law, where vocational training remained the guiding ethos. Most law professors and lecturers, like their students, were part-timers who combined teaching with practice, and this did not really change until the 1960s.

A real breakthrough in research had nevertheless occurred when the Carnegie Trust started work in the 1900s. Half its income was devoted to advancing research. It awarded scholarships and fellowships, financed research projects, and contributed to the cost of buildings and new posts. It was open to research proposals at a time when no similar funding was offered by the state. Otherwise the university still relied on wealthy individuals to finance new buildings or chairs. Edinburgh was less well placed than the new universities in northern England, or its rival in Glasgow, to tap into corporate wealth. The city lacked the sort of industries which created big fortunes, and if local magnates made contributions, they often preferred to finance projects of personal interest and prestige unrelated to their businesses. While William McEwan built the McEwan Hall, Alexander Bruce of the rival Younger brewing firm and the distiller Sir John Usher financed a chair of public health in 1898. Pasteur's visit in 1884 was said to have inspired this. Pasteur's work was certainly relevant to brewing and distilling, and the science of bacteriology was central to the new scientific medicine. But the new chair, and associated BSc degree, was more concerned with training experts for local government work than with basic research, and a chair of bacteriology was not established until 1913.

No other new medical chairs had been established since 1831, and the research achievements of that faculty remained modest as it struggled with a huge teaching load. The strong point of the medical school had always been advances in practical surgery. Surgeons like James Syme (1833–69), Joseph Lister (1869–77) and James Young Simpson (1840–70) became household names, and the influence of Edinburgh medical professors was spread through their authorship of standard textbooks and by the dispersal of their pupils throughout the world. Important work was done by the professors of physiology, John Hughes Bennett (1848–74) and Edward Sharpey Schafer

(1899–1933); but Edinburgh was not in the same research league as the great medical schools, lavishly funded by their governments, at Paris, Berlin or Vienna.

So too in science, geology in 1871 was the last new chair founded before the First World War, and while professors pursued their own original work, they were slow to develop research schools. This was true of Playfair, even though he had studied at Giessen under Justus Liebig, the great pioneer of the new approach, and neither he nor his successor Alexander Crum Brown (1869–1908), who was important in introducing the new organic chemistry to Britain, worked on the industrial applications of chemistry. The Professor of Natural Philosophy P. G. Tait (1860–1901) started a physics laboratory for his advanced students in 1868, but he was hostile to specialisation and strongly attached to the general educational role of his large lecture class. He had little use for science teaching in schools, claiming in 1888 that 'experience has led me to the deliberate conclusion that the *less* a man knows of Natural Philosophy when he enters my Ordinary Class, the better for

his progress in that fascinating study'. But the physics laboratories were expanded with a donation in 1900, and by that date the necessity of practical teaching in science was fully accepted.

The university was also handicapped in developing applied science and engineering by the creation of Heriot-Watt College in 1885, from an institution which went back to 1824 as a Mechanics' Institute. Heriot-Watt became the favoured channel for government aid to technical education. It was Heriot-Watt that actually developed courses in brewing, and by the 1900s it was supporting research and degree-level teaching in a number of specialities. Rather than trying to compete, the two institutions agreed to share the field of engineering. The university taught civil engineering, and the college mechanical and electrical engineering. In 1913 the college was formally affiliated to the university, so that its students could take Edinburgh degrees, and these joint arrangements worked amicably until Heriot-Watt was raised to full university status in the 1960s. When a chair of mining was endowed in 1924 by James Hood, a Midlothian coalowner (a rare example of a gift directly related to the donor's industry), the university was unable to offer teaching in the subject, and the chair was made a joint one with Heriot-Watt.

The research approach was slower to spread to arts subjects, particularly the traditional ones like classics and philosophy. Blackie, despite his advocacy of German scholarship, devoted his energies to his lectures and to public causes rather than to original research. In philosophy, continental trends like positivism (from France) and neo-idealism (from Germany) were resisted. For several decades both chairs were filled by clergymen, A. C. Fraser in logic (1856–91) and Henry Calderwood in moral philosophy (1868–97), who sought to keep alive the old Scottish 'commonsense' fusion of rationalism with religious belief. It was their successors, the confusingly named brothers Andrew Seth Pringle-Pattison (logic, 1891–1919) and James Seth (moral philosophy, 1898–1924), who brought Edinburgh into the largely neo-Hegelian mainstream of British university philosophy.

It was easier to innovate when new subjects were introduced. The first lecturers in German and French, promoted to chairs after the war, Otto Schlapp and Charles Sarolea respectively, made their students grapple with continental methods, while the diplomatic historian Richard Lodge and the first Professor of Scottish History, Peter Hume Brown – this chair was founded by a bequest in 1901 – based their advanced teaching on the detailed study of sources, and encouraged postgraduate research. A rather different approach was that of the successive professors of English literature, David Masson, George Saintsbury and Herbert Grierson, who moved away from the 'rhetoric' still embodied in the chair's title, but preferred the humane study of great authors to the narrow linguistic approach often found in British universities at this time. Something similar happened in music, elevated to a separate faculty in 1894. Although the Reid chair had existed since 1839, the professors had been mainly concerned with promoting the musical life of the university and the city, notably through the student Musical Society founded in the 1860s and the annual Reid Concert, which brought professional orchestras and star performers to the city. It was only with the appointment of Frederick Niecks in 1891 that the academic teaching of music really began. Niecks replaced the annual concert by a series of concerts, then of a novel kind, exploring musical history, and his successor in 1914, the pianist and eminent musicologist Donald Tovey, put the Edinburgh department firmly on the scholarly map.

Though the growth of the professorate before 1914 was limited, its composition underwent a significant change. Once scholarly or scientific achievement was the main criterion for appointment, Edinburgh became part of a national (and later international) market in academic posts. A chair in Edinburgh could be a stage in a career which started with a college fellowship at Oxford or Cambridge, passed through a chair at one of the new English university colleges, and might end by a return to England. The research criterion also made it difficult for laymen to judge the qualifications of candidates, or for political

and religious affiliations to count openly, so the real power over appointments returned from the Court, Curators, or crown to the University Senate. Until the 1870s, nearly all appointments were of Scots. However, between 1880 and 1914, of thirty-two professors appointed in the arts, science and music faculties, only fourteen were Scots, and several of those were in local specialities such as Celtic, Scottish history, and education. The law and divinity faculties remained Scottish strongholds for obvious reasons, and the medical faculty to a lesser extent because of the sense of a school with its own traditions. But in arts and science there was a significant 'anglicisation', though it actually included men born in Ireland, Wales and the British Empire, and two of German origin. Buoyant student numbers made Edinburgh chairs attractive to outsiders, offering high salaries and a comfortable lifestyle. In 1892 the direct levying of fees was abolished, and professors were paid fixed (but not equal) salaries. Most of them earned between £800 and £1,200 a year, which allowed them to occupy handsome flats in the West End, or villas in Newington and the Grange, and to count among the bourgeois elite of the city.

Equally significant was the growth of non-professorial staff.

Professors had always appointed assistants, paid from their fee income, and since 1858 a few had received salaries from public funds. In the 1880s, the university began to appoint permanent lecturers, initially to cover new specialities, which might later be converted into chairs, and then as posts under the direction of the professor. This was the origin of the modern 'department', and it was endorsed by the 1889 commission. Thereafter the number of lecturers and assistants, the latter usually on temporary contracts, grew steadily. The development of the non-professorial staff was consolidated after the First World

War when they gained a proper career structure (with senior lecturers and readers), a pension scheme, and representation on the Senate. A compulsory retiring age for professors (usually seventy) and the formation of the Scottish Association of University Teachers in 1922, later merged into an all-British Association of University Teachers, were other symptoms of change. In medicine, these developments tended to squeeze out the extra-mural lecturers, who also found it difficult to adapt to the move to laboratory teaching. In 1895 they grouped together as a School of Medicine linked with the two Royal Colleges, with its own laboratories. At that time there were over forty lecturers, but in later years their main clientele was overseas students, and they did not survive the formation of the National Health Service in 1948.

In 1884 the university had 38 professors, 3 lecturers and 26 assistants. In 1914 there were 43 professors, 87 lecturers, and over 100 assistants – giving a staff–student ratio of about 1:14. As with the development of research, this posed financial problems. The university was expected to introduce new subjects and more intensive teaching without a corresponding increase in fee income. In 1907–8, the university had a total income of £93,000, of which 53 per cent came from fees, 28 per cent from public sources, and 14 per cent from endowments. In 1910 the Scottish universities persuaded the Treasury to increase their grant, which had been unchanged since 1892. This boosted Edinburgh's income by 1913–14 to £115,000, and the public contribution to 36 per cent, but in return the universities agreed to charge a combined fee to students instead of separate fees for each course. The new fees were ten guineas a year for arts and twenty guineas for the BSc, reflecting the costs of laboratory teaching and equipment.

Scottish university education had been cheap because the universities were run on a shoestring. Large lecture courses were an economical method of teaching, and there was little in the way of administration or student support. There was a small clerical staff, mainly to deal with matriculation and finance, but only in the 1920s did the university create the posts of

The old Natural
Philosophy classroom,
taken in 1905 shortly
before the department
moved to High Schoo
Yards. (University of
Edinburgh)

University Accountant and University Secretary. Formerly
there were separate secretaries of Court and Senate, and these
posts were held by professors. Deans and heads of department
dealt with their own correspondence, usually in longhand. All
this was bound to change, but university education remained
cheap. Very roughly, the university was spending £38 per
student in 1914, of which the student paid half in fees. Over a
hundred years, prices have risen about sixty times, so the real
cost of a university education was, in current terms, £2,200,
and the fee paid by the student £1,100. (In 2000 the 'full fee'
paid by overseas students was £7,210 for non-laboratory
subjects, £9,480 for science and medicine.) Changes in relative
income make this calculation a rather notional one, but in
1914, when even the most prosperous workers were unlikely to
earn more than £2 a week, an annual fee of £15–20, combined
with living expenses of perhaps a pound a week over thirty
weeks, was enough to debar poorer students without bursaries.
Fortunately these were fairly numerous, though capricious in
their dependence on local links and special qualifications.

Many observers thought that before 1914 the university had a leisured stateliness which was never recaptured. Nostalgia apart, the war certainly had a profound effect on Edinburgh, as on all universities. Young men volunteered en masse, even before the imposition of conscription in 1915. The number of male students declined sharply, and many came only for a year or so, hoping to complete their degrees after war service. It was only in medicine that the authorities encouraged men to complete their degrees. This meant that the proportion of women rose, allowing them to play a much more prominent part in university affairs, providing a senior president of the SRC for the first time, Agnes Cunningham in 1915–16. Women engaged in various types of war work, such as sewing and knitting for the troops, nursing, entertaining visiting soldiers, and fundraising for the Scottish Women's Hospitals founded by Dr Elsie Inglis in Serbia and France. The Women's Suffrage Society, founded in 1909, threw itself into these war activities, though it was to be dissolved when the vote was achieved for women over thirty in 1918. The total number of women rose too, from 552 in 1913–14 to over a thousand in 1919–20. This was due partly to the final acceptance of women in the medical faculty in 1916, and there was a remarkable boom in women medical students – there were over 400 immediately after the war, compared with 150 or fewer in the late 1920s. The First World War was less decisive for the emancipation of women than has sometimes been claimed, but the old restrictions on their social lives were swept away, and there was no return to the somewhat marginal position occupied by 'lady students' before 1914.

Nearly 8,000 Edinburgh students and graduates served in the armed forces, and 944 were killed – about 12 per cent, a figure typical for British universities. Naturally the proportion was higher for the immediate pre-war generations, and the memory of these losses overhung the two following decades. The university's war memorial, designed by Sir Robert Lorimer, was inaugurated in 1923. Meanwhile the survivors had returned in large numbers to complete their studies, and

War work in the Chemistry laboratory, 1915. (University of Edinburgh, Chemistry Museum)

Charles Barkla, Professor of Natural Philosophy, with graduates, 1918. Of the ten BSc graduates in Pure Science in 1918, seven were women. (University of Edinburgh)

for several years after the war every part of the university bulged at the seams. The medical faculty, which had 1,304 students in 1913–14, had to cope with 1,968 in 1919–20 and 1,967 in 1920–1, when the university as a whole reached a record attendance of 4,886.

Once the ex-servicemen had passed through, enrolments settled at a lower level, but remained above 4,000 in most years until 1934. In the 1930s, however, there was stagnation and some decline, and a sense of malaise and financial crisis was in the air. The celebrations of the university's 350th anniversary in 1933 were muted compared with 1884. The university suffered from the economic depression, and specifically from the cuts in education which were the government's response to the crisis of 1931. Teaching posts in schools became fewer and less well paid, and this particularly affected women, for whom teaching was the main career choice. The percentage of women reached a peacetime peak of 31 in 1924–5 (compared with 17 on the eve of war), but declined in the 1930s, to 24 in 1938–9. Stagnancy of university numbers can also be related to the continuing conservatism of Scottish educational policy. Hopes of a greater democratisation of secondary education in 1918 were disappointed. In 1936 schools were reorganised to make all post-primary education 'secondary', but this did not have time to take effect before 1939. The inter-war years did see some expansion of local-authority scholarships for working-class children, but not on a scale which changed the fundamental social character of the system.

One effect of the First World War was to underline the importance of science to the strength of the nation, and the duty of the state to support it. Edinburgh's own scientific contributions to the war effort seem to have been modest. Alfred Ewing, who was appointed Principal in 1916, was an Edinburgh engineering graduate and later a professor in several universities. In 1914 he was Director of Naval Education, and became famous as the 'Man in Room 40' who developed the navy's cryptography services, but this work was largely complete before he came to Edinburgh. During the war the government set up the Department of Scientific and Industrial Research, the ancestor of the modern research councils, through which the state began to invest in research. From 1919, the annual grants to Scottish universities, increased to allow for wartime inflation, were channelled through the new University Grants Committee (UGC). In principle at least, there was now a national policy-making body, though the UGC had a 'hands-off' approach intended to preserve university autonomy, and was cautious in giving directions.

The annual UGC grant was increased regularly, and continued to contribute about a third of the university's revenue. Student fees were raised by a modest amount, and the univer-

King's Buildings in 1933. From front to back, the Chemistry, Geology and Zoology buildings. The statue o Brewster has been moved here. Photographs capture the raw character of th site in its early years.

Students on a Biological Society field trip to Barra, 1936. Better-off students could afford cars. (University of Edinburgh)

sity balanced its books, but as before 1914 innovations depended almost entirely on private money, and new efforts were made to tap outside sources of wealth. An Alumnus (later Graduates') Association was started in 1924, and from 1925 the *University of Edinburgh Journal* kept the far-flung graduates in touch with current developments. There were alumni clubs throughout the world, and the 1933 anniversary was marked by the holding of simultaneous dinners. The one in Melbourne was presided over by David Orme Masson, Professor of Chemistry there, who had been the first Senior President of the SRC in 1884. The anniversary was also marked by a 'world

University of Edinburgh

Opening of the New Extension to the Surgical Research Department, 20th July 1938. By the Right Hon. Walter Elliot Minister of Health

message' from Principal Holland, broadcast by the BBC.

In the optimistic climate of the immediate post-war years, the university made ambitious plans. By 1931, the arts faculty acquired new chairs in French, German, archaeology, psychology and geography, as well as the two business chairs already mentioned. In medicine chairs were founded in tuberculosis (held by Robert Philip, a noted pioneer in the battle against the disease), therapeutics, psychiatry, and child life and health. In science, there were chairs in mining, forestry, and animal genetics, along with second chairs in zoology and natural philosophy. The boldest move was the acquisition in 1919 of the greenfield site at Liberton, on which the King's Buildings were constructed as a science campus. The first building completed was for chemistry (1922), followed by zoology (1929) and geology in 1932. The Institute of Animal Genetics opened in 1930: this was a subject in which Edinburgh was a pioneer, having had a lectureship in genetics since 1911. It arose from the interest of the Professor of Zoology, James Cossar Ewart, in animal breeding. Francis Crew became lecturer in 1921, and support from the Scottish Board of Agriculture and the Empire Marketing Board allowed him to be given a chair in 1928. Sheep were a special interest from the start, and at that time there was enough space on the King's Buildings site for a thirty-acre experimental farm.

Natural Philosophy and engineering remained, and expanded, in the central area at High School Yards, where they had moved before the war. New buildings for science were financed by a mixture of appeal money and donations from businessmen, but as usual their gifts were seldom related to their own businesses, and direct help from industry was almost non-existent. Laurence Pullar, a member of the Perth dyeing dynasty, gave £20,000 for zoology, the Galashiels tweed manufacturer James Sanderson bequeathed £50,000 for new engineering laboratories, and the Edinburgh biscuit magnate Sir Alexander Grant (no relation of the former Principal) gave £50,000 for Geology. The Carnegie foundation remained an important funder, but post-war reconstruction also brought the great American foundations on to the European scene, and the Rockefeller Foundation (earlier known as the International Education Board) gave £74,000 of the £112,000 cost of the zoology building, £30,000 for animal genetics, and other large sums for medical education. But in the 1930s the flow of gifts slowed down, and no new chairs were founded after 1931 – apart from the four added in 1932 after the reunion of the Scottish churches in 1929: the established church merged with the United Free Church, itself formed in 1900 by the union of the Free and United Presbyterian Churches. New College, the old Free Church foundation on the Mound, now became the home of the university's divinity faculty. The newly reunited church retained a say in the appointment of divinity professors.

The men who returned from the trenches in 1918 and 1919 were determined to enjoy themselves, and there was a new enthusiasm in the 1920s for 'corporate life'. The old forms of student activity revived, and there was an important new one, the annual charities week in aid of hospitals and other good causes, notably the University Settlement, which had been

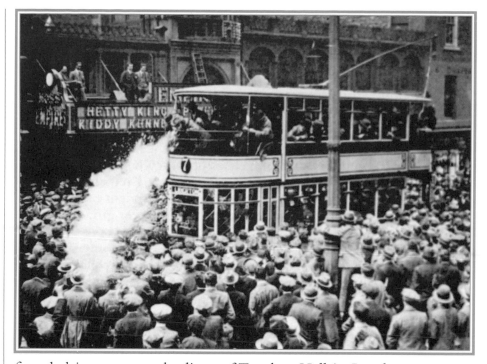

founded in 1905, on the lines of Toynbee Hall in London, to provide recreation, social services and adult education to the poor of the South Side. Charities week did not take on a definitive form, directly organised by the SRC, until 1932, but its main features were established earlier. The centrepiece was a float parade and street collection, accompanied from 1928 by the sale of a supposedly comic magazine. There were all kinds of ancillary activities, and some older traditions such as torchlight processions and theatrical revues were now concentrated around the event. But throughout the year there were new opportunities for urban leisure and for contact with the opposite (and for some, no doubt, the same) sex. Dance halls, picture-houses and tea-rooms all became student haunts. Between the wars the cinema and dancing provided most students with their relaxation, and unlike student politics, journalism or team games, they were as open to women as to men. The 'Union Palais' on Saturday nights became one of the most popular dances in Edinburgh, though Union membership itself remained firmly masculine and medical, and a separate Women's Union continued.

Women could also participate as equals in some of the newer forms of physical recreation. New games appeared, such as lacrosse (for women), basketball (played by American medical students), judo and badminton (but not yet squash). Tennis took on new life with the opening of courts at King's Buildings. Field athletics, neglected since the early days of the Athletic Club, were revived after the war, and scored a notable triumph when Eric Liddell won a gold medal, and set a world record, in the 400 metres at the 1924 Olympic Games. More novel was the popularity of non-competitive outdoor activities such as camping, hiking, cycling, climbing, yachting and skiing. The cult of the healthy outdoors was part of the atmosphere of these years, and so was a new national concern with physical fitness. Both the UGC and the Carnegie fund were willing to give grants for social and athletic purposes, and Carnegie gave £15,000 in 1920, used mainly to buy the Canal Field at Craiglockhart. In 1924 the Scottish SRCs urged the universi-

ties to add a compulsory levy for student activities to the
matriculation fee. In 1926, Edinburgh set up a committee of
inquiry on physical education under the Rector's assessor, Lord
Constable, and its main recommendations were implemented
in 1929–30. These included the replacement of the old Field
Committee by a more comprehensive Athletics Committee, a
levy of 10s 6d on each student paid into a Physical Welfare
Fund, systematic medical inspection, and the appointment of a
Director of Physical Training. However, its recommendation
that 'it should be a point of honour with every member of the
staff to countenance and encourage by his frequent presence
the athletic activities of the students' probably fell on less recep-
tive ground.

The new Director was Colonel Ronald Campbell, an army gymnastics expert and a champion boxer and Olympic fencer. From his base at a newly fitted-up gymnasium at Minto House in Chambers Street, Campbell waged war on slackers. In 1932–3 he observed that out of 2,899 male students, only 479 belonged to the Athletic Club (which continued to coordinate team sports), and another 218 attended PT classes. Others prac- tised sport outside the university, but Campbell estimated that there were still 1,700 or so couch potatoes, who forgot that 'the body is the sheet-anchor of the brain'. In 1936 he reminded them that 'the fitter the body the better it will enable the brain to play the game before it – football or final examinations', and pointed out that 'the games-playing student becomes a good mixer, a quality which will help him in after-life'. Campbell introduced Physical Efficiency Tests to allow a graded system of instruction and the award of certificates. He thought that 'Physical Education can be made to expand into the realms of ethics and become inspired with a philosophy of its own.' His ideal would have been to make it compulsory, but though the university agreed to Campbell's Certificate of Physical Proficiency in 1938, said to be the first in Britain, compulsion would have been a step too far in Scotland.

The OTC was among the student activities revived after the war – by 1925 it was up to 351 members – but it could hardly be as uncontroversially patriotic as before. The political views of Edinburgh students await their historian, but the university was never insulated from national issues. There had been a short-lived Socialist Society in the 1880s, and a Fabian Society founded in 1897 was active until after the war. A university Labour Party was formed in 1922, but its renaming as the Socialist Society in 1935 indicated the tensions within the British (and especially Scottish) left. The rise of fascism and the Spanish civil war certainly had a strong impact on students, not all in a leftward direction, as did nationalism: a Scottish Nationalist Association was formed in 1928, but did not have the same impact on rectorial elections as at Glasgow and Aberdeen. The sculptor Pittendrigh MacGillivray stood as a nationalist in 1932, and C. M. Grieve, the poet Hugh Mac-Diarmid, in 1935 and 1936, but they received very few votes.

More popular between the wars was an idealistic internationalism. A League of Nations Society was formed in 1920 and an International Club in 1927. In the 1920s and 1930s, the League of Nations attracted wide support, for while only a small minority embraced pacifist views, or criticised the OTC as 'militarist', the longing for a peaceful world was deeply felt among students, who feared that they would be the sacrificed generation in a new war. There were also greater formal links with students elsewhere. An International Academic Committee had been set up by the SRC as early as 1892, and had specialised in providing information and welfare services for overseas students coming to Scotland, including a system of contacts in foreign universities known as 'academic consuls'. But after the war the Scottish SRCs joined the International Confederation of Students (CIE), a mainly European body, and for this purpose constituted the National Union of Scottish Students. Cheap travel and accommodation, as well as exchange visits in both directions, followed from this.

If the election of rectors is any guide, conventional political allegiances remained thoroughly conservative, as students also showed by strike-breaking activities in 1919 and during the 1926 General Strike. Kitchener had been elected in 1914, and he was followed until 1935 by a succession of military men, war leaders and Unionist politicians: Admiral Beatty in 1917, Lloyd George in 1920, Baldwin in 1923, Sir John Gilmour in 1926 (he was a former Conservative Scottish secretary: this was the last election accompanied by the traditional battle), Churchill in 1929, General Sir Ian Hamilton in 1932, Field-Marshal Allenby in 1935. These confined themselves to the traditional oration. But in the 1930s there was a demand in all the Scottish universities for non-political rectors, and indeed for 'working rectors' who would chair the Court. In 1930 the graduates chose Sir James Barrie, the leading Scottish man of letters, to replace A. J. Balfour as Chancellor, and in 1936, following Allenby's death, the students elected Herbert Grierson, the retiring Professor of English Literature, as Rector. Grierson used his inaugural speech to reassert the values of liberal education, and to condemn the failure of many students to acquire it since specialisation had taken over: there was 'something melancholy in the plight of the professional man or scientific specialist who has no resources outside his profession or subject beyond golf, bridge, and perhaps the novels of P. G. Wodehouse'.

In 1939, Grierson was succeeded by Sir Donald Pollock, one of the university's greatest benefactors. Pollock was a medical graduate of 1893 who had made his fortune by shipbreaking –

notably by salvaging the German fleet sunk at Scapa Flow. Pollock bought up and donated land and buildings in the Pleasance (where the new Pollock Gymnasium was opened in 1940, part of a longer-term plan for the extension of sports facilities) and in the area between Old College and George Square, which was to be vital to the university's post-war expansion. In 1942–3 he gave the land on which the Pollock Halls were to be built. These benefactions were made through a trust which Pollock controlled, and he took a close interest in how they were used, in ways often thought obstructive by the university authorities. He also acted as a working rector, chairing the Court and cultivating relations with students. The first new hall on the Pollock site was not opened, however, until 1960, and pre-war Edinburgh remained essentially non-residential. The main innovation was the opening of Cowan House in George Square in 1929, a hall for men to complement Masson Hall, financed by the shipowner Thomas Cowan of Leith, as a thank-offering for students' volunteer efforts in the General Strike.

The Second World War in some ways had less impact on university life than the First. Conscription was imposed from the start, but students were not called up until they were twenty and so could start work on their degrees. The university was also much used by the services for intensive short courses. Thus overall student numbers remained at the pre-war level, though, as in 1914, the proportion of women students rose. The most unusual development was the creation of the Polish Medical School, to serve the needs of the Polish army which had taken refuge in Britain; it continued for a few years after the war as students completed their courses. In the long run, the significance of the 1939–45 war was that it created new expectations for social justice and equality of opportunity, which, unlike those of 1918, were to be largely fulfilled in the ensuing decades.

CHAPTER 4

Age of Expansion

Since 1945 the scale and complexity of the university's activities has increased enormously, but little of this has yet been investigated by historians. It would be impossible in a short space to give an adequate account of changes in the curriculum, developments in the main disciplines, or unfolding events. At best, one can give some idea of the 'public' aspects of the university's life, and its relationship with the broader evolution of the university system. For this period was marked not just by numerical expansion, but by a closer relationship with the state, and the University of Edinburgh's identity was increasingly defined by its place in the social and intellectual hierarchy of British universities.

The expansion of British universities after the Second World War is commonly associated with the Robbins committee, which reported in 1963. But Robbins only endorsed trends already well under way. Even before the war ended, it became national policy to expand higher education, especially in science and technology, and in the 1940s and 1950s this growth was expected to take place within existing universities rather than through new foundations. In the late 1930s, Edinburgh's enrolments were around 4,000, but by 1948–9 there were 5,640 full-time students. In part this was a post-war bulge of the kind experienced after 1918, and numbers stabilised for a time, falling to 4,537 in 1953–4, but they then began to rise steadily. Between 1960–1 and 1970–1 they rose from 5,963 to 9,368. The 1960s were the period of most rapid expansion, after which pressure on the older universities was eased as new ones were founded – Heriot-Watt achieved university status in 1966, ending the longstanding arrangements for joint teaching – and expansion was directed into other parts of what was now called 'tertiary' education. The 1970s and 1980s were a new period of stability: having reached 9,193 in 1968–9, it took twenty years for enrolments to drift upwards to 10,403 in 1988–9. But in the 1990s growth resumed, reaching 18,000 before the absorption of Moray House College of Education, decided in 1998, brought the total to over 20,000.

Most of this expansion was determined by government policy, which was itself responding to wider social trends such as the post-war baby boom, the democratisation of secondary education, the extension of graduate status to an increasing number of occupations, and the changing social expectations of women. Equal opportunities for women, though perhaps ultimately a result of the social revolution stimulated by the war, did not really make their impact until the late 1960s and 1970s. Before the war, as we have seen, the percentage of women in the university was higher in the 1920s (31 per cent in 1924–5) than in the 1930s (24 per cent in 1938–9). In the 1940s and 1950s there was only slight change, the percentage varying between 25 and 29. It reached 30 again in 1962–3, then jumped to 36 in 1967–8, and rose steadily to 45 in 1980–1. Throughout the 1980s and 1990s it remained in the range 45–48 per cent, until the merger with Moray House allowed women students to overtake men.

There were those in the 1960s who feared that a larger university would lose its identity, but there could be no resisting the demands of the state, which now held the financial whiphand. Before the 1939–45 war some 36 per cent of the university's income came from the state – as it had since 1910. About 32 per cent came from student fees, and 17 percent from endowments, with a balance from miscellaneous sources. But post-war governments were prepared to fund universities generously, and by 1952–3, 73 per cent of the university's income came as a direct grant from the UGC. It remained at this level until the end of the 1970s. The second largest source of income was research grants, many of which also came from the state via the research councils. Existing endowments lost much of their value through inflation, and appealing for new

ones was a less urgent priority (though it was not neglected)
now that the state seemed willing to pay for academic expansion, and for student accommodation and social facilities, as
soon as new needs were established. Student fees, too, still a
significant element in university income in the 1950s, were
normally paid by the state from the 1960s; they were not raised
in line with real costs, and dwindled to 4 or 5 per cent of total
income in the 1970s. All of this, in retrospect, made the university dangerously dependent on the goodwill of politicians.

In the Robbins era universities had a central role in plans to
modernise Britain and make its economy internationally
competitive. Investment in science and technology, which had
emerged from the war with new prestige, seemed a national
priority. One of those involved in post-war scientific planning,
the Nobel prizewinning physicist Edward Appleton, became

Principal in 1949, and he and his successor Michael Swann (1965–73, after being professor of Natural History since 1952) laid foundations for Edinburgh's later scientific prosperity. Edinburgh did not have much share in the glamorous 'big science' of the 1950s, nuclear physics, but it became a pioneer in the two crucial fields of electronics and computer science, and genetics and molecular biology. But science was by no means the only area of growth and investment. The formation of the National Health Service in 1948 required a complete overhaul of the relationship between medical teaching and the hospital service, including the absorption of the previously independent Edinburgh Dental School. Medical students were now a much smaller element in the student body than in the nineteenth century – only 8 per cent by 2000 – but teaching them was disproportionately expensive. In all subjects, indeed, teaching became more complex and intensive. The Robbins committee criticised the Scottish universities for relying too much on lectures and neglecting small-group teaching. To remedy this required both lower staff–student ratios – 1:8 was regarded as the ideal at this time – and investment in libraries and other student support services. As student numbers grew, so did staff, especially in the non-professorial grades. In 1937–8, the university had 44 professors and 133 other academic staff – a total of 177. But after the war, the intimacy of the academic community was lost: total staff rose to 501 in 1954–5 and 750 in 1963–4, and then doubled to 1,500 by 1978–9. Although staff-student ratios worsened in later years, expansion contin-ued, and there were some 3,000 academic staff by 2000.

Appleton and Swann believed that university education should bridge the gap between science and the humanities, and left a monument to this ideal in the Appleton Tower at George Square, designed to ensure that science students spent their first year in company with arts students rather than at King's Buildings. But in fact increasing specialisation was a marked feature of the post-war years. The Scottish generalist ideal, despite a powerful polemical defence by George Davie in his book *The Democratic Intellect* (1961), could not be sustained

Bedside manner: clinical instruction, c. 1960. (Edinburgh University Library, Special Collections)

The Staff Club in Chambers Street opened in 1960. It was a popular facility for many years, but fell victim to changing social habits in the 1990s. The wall painting was by Leonard Rosoman. (Edinburgh University Library, Special Collections)

against the pressures, both academic and vocational, favouring specialisation. This was most apparent in the arts faculty. In 1964–5 two-thirds of graduates were still taking the Ordinary degree, but this was to change rapidly: ten years later the balance between the Honours and the general degree was equal, and the decline of the latter continued thereafter, resisting all attempts to refurbish its attractions. Equally significant, though less noticed, was the virtual disappearance from the

MA of science subjects and the once popular mathematics and natural philosophy Honours group. There were similar trends in the BSc itself and in the social sciences degree. This caused yet further pressure on teaching resources, as four years of study again became the norm, and the numbers in Honours classes increased.

The rise of the social sciences was another striking post-war development. Subjects like geography and economics had long been taught, and there were modest inter-war developments in business studies and in training for social work. Now a new conceptual approach which separated social science subjects from the humanities, coupled with a move towards graduate status for professions like accountancy and nursing, led to the creation of a separate faculty, hived off from arts in 1965. Edinburgh was a pioneer in making nursing into a graduate subject – the chair created in 1971 was said to be the first in Europe – though for those unfamiliar with the nuances of the medical profession it is unclear why it should be considered a social science rather than a branch of medicine. Much social science teaching was vocational, but the period also saw the development of more purely academic subjects such as politics, sociology and social anthropology, which attracted students even though, or because, they were not taught in schools. Social anthropology became the base for another Edinburgh speciality, the study of race relations; this was supported by the Nuffield Foundation – one of its grants, in 1954–5, was to study 'racial problems in the Brixton area of London'. The social sciences faculty soon equalled the science faculty (and differed from arts) in its high proportion of postgraduates, due largely to the growth of vocational diplomas alongside doctoral work.

Before the war, postgraduates had formed less than 10 per cent of the university's students, but by the 1950s they had risen to around 15 per cent, at which level they remained until the 1990s. This was one important change in the composition of the student body. Another was the advent of selection and national recruitment. Before the war, anyone who could meet the entrance requirement could matriculate in the university, and most faculties did not see any need to limit numbers. The cost of studying and the limited availability of bursaries and grants put natural limits on recruitment, and the university continued to draw on its traditional catchment areas. This continued in the early post-war years. But the Anderson report of 1960 – as important in its way as Robbins – recommended that all British students who gained a university place should have their fees paid by the state and should receive a means-tested grant to cover the cost of living away from home. This remarkably generous proposal was accepted by the government. Admissions were now organised through a national clearing house, and students made multiple applications; Edinburgh faculties found that they had ten or more applicants for every place, and had to devise entrance mechanisms. Slowly but surely – more slowly in Scotland than elsewhere, but more rapidly at Edinburgh than at Glasgow or Aberdeen – the universities became detached from their regional roots, and pupils in Edinburgh schools began to think of going anywhere but to their local university.

In 1950, as before the war, about half of the university's students had their 'domicile' within thirty miles of Edinburgh. By 1964–5, this had fallen to 37 per cent. This statistic does not exist for later years, but a comparable one was for students living at home: these were still 30 per cent in 1967–8, but thereafter fell steadily, to 17 per cent at the end of the century. Moreover, English students began to replace Scottish ones. In 1980, 70 per cent of undergraduates came from Scotland, 26 per cent from the rest of the United Kingdom, and four percent from overseas. (The university was more 'Scottish' at this time than in 1880, when the comparable figures were 65, 21 and 14.) However, in the 1980s and 1990s the balance steadily shifted, and by 1997, only 42 per cent were Scottish, 48 per cent coming from the rest of the United Kingdom, and 10 per cent from overseas.

Until the huge building programme in the 1960s, which transformed the face of the university, overcrowding of facili-

Both academic and social facilities were badly overcrowded in the 1960s. Above: Library Reading Room in the former Natural History Museum. After the Library moved to George Square, this became the Talbot Rice Arts Centre. Below: Lunch break in the student common room. This is the lower hall beneath the old Museum. It was later converted into a Senate Hall, and later still the Senatus was ejected to make way for offices. (University of Edinburgh)

ties was an everyday feature of university life. Even before the war there were plans for physical expansion, and there was some talk after it of giving up King's Buildings and reintegrating the university on a central site. But this was impractical, and expansion at King's Buildings was on a large scale in the 1960s, notably in the multi-phase James Clerk Maxwell Building, which allowed the Physics and Mathematics departments to move from the central area as well as accommodating the Computer Science department and the Edinburgh Regional Computing Centre, set up in 1966. Once this phase of building was complete in the mid-1970s, all the science departments were housed at King's Buildings. The other area of expansion, George Square, was more controversial as it involved the demolition of a large swathe of existing buildings. On the square itself, many houses had already been converted to university purposes, and there had been new building, for the Agriculture and Forestry departments, as early as 1914. Most of George Square was now designated for the main arts and social science buildings and the University Library, and the Bristo area to the north of it for student facilities. These plans were pushed through despite the opposition of conservationists, and mostly completed by 1970. The university also sponsored a Comprehensive Development Area, which would have destroyed almost all the surrounding residential and commercial buildings. Fortunately, these plans were not carried out, but during this complex saga the university often seemed insensitive and arrogant, and suffered from growing public feeling against the destruction of inner-city communities, and over the conservation of older buildings, even when these were not of outstanding architectural merit.

In the end the university itself contributed to the conservationist cause, by such schemes as the renovation of Mylne's Court, on Lawnmarket, as a student residence. The post-war years saw large-scale construction on the Pollock Halls site, initially in the form of traditional halls with refectories and high tables. Student preferences soon turned against this formality, and later developments provided for self-catering. There were nearly 2,000 places on the site by 1970. However, the virtual disappearance of the Edinburgh landlady, combined with the growing number of students from outside Edinburgh, caused a persistent accommodation crisis in the 1970s. Apart from the Pollock site, the university responded by building smaller student houses, and for a time by leasing hard-to-let council accommodation in Wester Hailes and even in

Aerial view looking south, c. 1983. Old College in the foreground, the McEwan Hall to the right, George Square behind it. The gap site in the centre used as a car park was intended for a new dental hospital, but this project was cancelled in 1989. Until the site is filled, the post-war dream of an integrated university precinct remains incomplete. (University of Edinburgh)

Livingston. An Accommodation Service was set up in 1973 to help students find flats, and in the long run the shift from digs to living independently in shared flats was one of the biggest changes in student life. By 2000, only a handful of students lived in traditional lodgings with meals provided, while 17 per cent lived in their own or their parents' home, as we have seen (many of these being mature students), 31 per cent in university accommodation, and 50 per cent in flats or bedsits. This shift coincided with the emergence of the city, surprisingly to its older inhabitants, as a hedonistic centre of fashionable bars and nightlife. Though most students now came from outside Edinburgh, they were engaging in new ways with the everyday life of the city.

But in the 1960s this was in the future, and the problems of student housing, overcrowding and discipline in residential halls were among the reasons for the student disturbances of

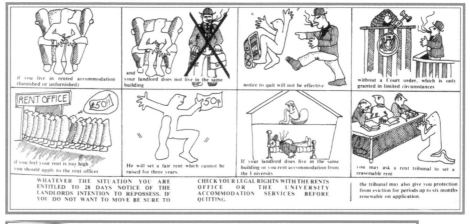

the early 1970s. The ideal of an intimate community of scholars still put forth in official rhetoric did not match the more anonymous and mechanistic reality which students encountered on their arrival. The 'youth revolt' of the 1960s and the liberalisation of social and sexual mores which accompanied it were universal phenomena; one local symptom was that ritualised rowdyism of the sort connected with rectorials died out in the 1960s – it had only made sense in the context of behaviour that was normally conventional and conformist. The forms of corporate life developed in the late nineteenth century had aimed essentially at inculcating the social mores of the professional classes. Students were the youthful segment of the middle class. Now they became the middle-class segment

A meeting of the SRC in 1963–4. On the left, Senior President George Foulkes. (University of Edinburgh, SRC)

of youth, and shared in a common generational culture during their university years. This was expressed in the way students dressed, and in their musical tastes; the portable record-player, the transistor radio and the disco, which emancipated dancing from live bands, helped to transform the student way of life.

Student revolt was an international phenomenon in the 1960s. At Edinburgh the main unrest occurred not in the famous year 1968, but a few years later, and focused on the institution of the rectorship. It was in many ways a very orthodox form of politics, and student leaders were not drawn from the extra-parliamentary left, as in some British universities, but from the political parties, mainly but not exclusively Labour. They had close links with conventional Scottish politics, and many militants later became councillors, MPs or journalists. The university's interests may well have suffered from their memories of the inept handling of student issues in the 1970s.

After the war there was a tendency in the Scottish universities to choose actors and comedians as rectors. The Edinburgh-born actor Alastair Sim served in 1948–51 and James Robertson Justice in 1957–60. After a return to orthodoxy with the election of the Liberal leader Jo Grimond, Justice was

Traditional student
activities continued to
flourish: two images
from 1977. Above: a
hockey team at the
Folkestone Festival.
Below: Bill and Ben
the Flowerpot Men
with Weed, during
Charities Week.
(University of
Edinburgh,
The Student)

re-elected in 1963–6. He was a man of distinctly left-wing
views, but his appeal was no doubt enhanced, especially for
medical students, by his portrayal of the testy surgeon Sir
Lancelot Sprat in the *Doctor in the House* films. His successor in
1966, Malcolm Muggeridge, was expected to be an equally
humorous figure, as a former editor of *Punch*, but proved not to
be. A stern Christian moralist, he resigned in 1968 over the
installation of a contraceptive machine in the Union. The

What do you mean, it's Malcolm Muggeridge's fault?

wider significance of the issue was that the students expected
the Rector to act as their representative, while Muggeridge
rejected this role. Student representation on university bodies,
especially the Court, was to become the flashpoint of conflict.
Following the student troubles in England, the Committee of
Vice-Chancellors and the National Union of Students had
agreed a 'concordat' on student representation. However, senior
members of the university, brought up in the autocratic profes-

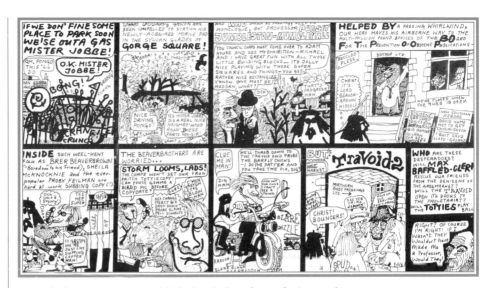

The adventures of Gaston le Jobbe (in beret). Among those caricatured are Percy Johnson-Marshall, Professor of Urban Design and Regional Planning, and consultant for the university's Development Plan; student politicians Gordon Brown and Sheila McKechnie; and Max Stafford-Clark, director of the Traverse Theatre. The Traverse, then in the Grassmarket, was a noted bohemian haunt.
(Courtesy of Jonathan Wills)

sorial departments which had developed since the 1890s, were seldom inclined to defer to the views of students, or indeed of the younger staff, who had recently joined the university in such numbers and who shared the mood of the age. Principal Swann was a man of conservative cast: he was the only Scottish contributor to the three *Black Papers* of 1969–70, which put forward a radical-right educational agenda. Swann was supported by the University Secretary, Charles Stewart, an extremely able administrator, but one who had been in his post since 1948.

Tensions between the Court and students developed during the rectorship of the distinguished journalist and environmentalist Kenneth Allsop (1969–72). Greater student representation was part of his platform. The university was willing to allow this for purely student matters, but resisted students' claim to take part in decision-making on policy questions such as the university's investments in firms with South African links – a well-chosen issue, as questions of racism and world poverty aroused wide student interest, corresponding to the internationalist idealism of the inter-war years. This period saw various sit-ins and student occupations, and feelings were exacerbated by a strip-cartoon in *The Student*, drawn by Jonathan Wills, depicting the adventures of the layabout student Gaston le Jobbe. This contained amusing but often vicious caricatures of

senior university figures, especially Swann and Stewart. Thus, it was no recipe for harmony when Wills was elected as Allsop's successor. As a postgraduate student, he was the first student Rector in Scotland. Wills resigned after a year, but was succeeded by another postgraduate, Gordon Brown (1973–6). Brown focused on the constitutional issues, already a matter of acrimonious dispute under Allsop and Wills, of the Rector's right to chair the Court and to appoint his own assessor, and it required legal action to confirm these rights; the authorities fought back with plans for an Ordinance to debar the Rector from chairing the Court. Normal relations returned only after the election of the affable television personality Magnus Magnusson as Brown's successor, and the retirement of Stewart in 1978 (Swann had already gone in 1973). The university

withdrew the Ordinance on the chairmanship, and subsequent
rectors generally did chair the Court, but changes were enacted
in 1977 which debarred students from election and extended
the electorate to staff as well as students. More importantly,
there were to be guaranteed places for student officers on the
Court, and similar arrangements were made for representation
on the Senatus and faculties. Although there were some further
student disturbances in the 1970s, these concessions largely
defused student revolt, and their acceptance at an earlier stage
might have avoided much trouble.

These internal problems were a distraction from mounting
difficulties on the financial front. The financial bonanza set off
by the Robbins report lasted for barely a decade. Governments
were alarmed by their open-ended commitment to increase
student numbers, and came to believe that universities were
wastefully run, while the rapid inflation of the 1970s caused
severe planning problems: between 1969–70 and 1980–1,
although the number of students hardly changed, the total
expenditure of the university rose from £10.9 million to £57.9
million. The proportion contributed by the Exchequer grant
remained above 70 per cent for most of this period, but from
1976 it started on a downward trend. By 1973–4 the univer-

sity's annual report was speaking of a 'financial blizzard' affecting all universities. 'Stringent' measures had to be adopted, including leaving posts vacant and encouraging the early retirement of staff. But this was only a prelude to the policy of exposing universities to market pressures initiated by the Thatcher government of 1979, with its ideological coolness towards the public sector. In 1981 the UGC implemented a set of severe cuts Principal Burnett claimed (not necessarily correctly) that the university faced its gravest financial crisis for two hundred years, though two years later he felt able to report that it was 'battered but intact' despite the loss of 300 academic posts. This formula might well have been used at other times during the financial fluctuations of subsequent years, which included an internally generated crisis in 1990. Disaster was always avoided, but coping with the constantly changing demands of the funding authorities became a permanent preoccupation for those in charge of policy.

Changes in funding were also linked with reorganisation of the higher education system. A series of changes between 1988 and 1992 resulted in the designation of most institutions of higher education as universities, ending the former 'binary' system. In principle, all were now funded on the same basis, but in practice governments sought to discriminate between institutions by reducing the core grant and providing other funds according to various discretionary formulae. Universities were encouraged to diversify by increasing fee income (which meant recruiting more overseas students) and by maximising research grants. A university with a strong research record like Edinburgh was well placed to profit from such a system, but it involved far more active management than before. In the 1970s, over 70 per cent of income still came from the block grant. By 2000 the equivalent source only provided 38 per cent, while fee income had been pushed up to 14 per cent and research grants to 25 per cent; endowment income was now only 3 per cent, but various forms of revenue-earning filled the gap of 20 per cent.

There was a further financial complication, and a dilemma

in defining the university's identity. When the Scottish Parliament was set up in 1999, universities came under its control, and funds were channelled through the Scottish Higher Education Funding Council, though often determined by UK-wide funding criteria. As a major research university, should Edinburgh see itself as an elite institution within the Scottish system, or cultivate its links with other British universities of the same status? In its mission statement at the beginning of the new century, the university declared itself to be both 'a leading European centre of academic excellence', sustaining and developing 'its identity as a research and teaching institution of the highest international quality', and 'a great civic university' which 'values its intellectual and economic relationship with the Scottish community that forms its base'. Ever since its foundation, the university has balanced its obligations to the city, the nation, the Empire, the international academic community. But when fewer than half of its students come from Scotland, and the once close links with local schools have all but dissolved, the community base is perhaps the part of the balance most in need of attention.

SELECT BIBLIOGRAPHY

GENERAL WORKS

Birse, R. M., *Engineering at Edinburgh University: A Short History, 1673–1983* (1983)

Birse, R. M., *Science at the University of Edinburgh, 1583–1993* (1994)

Bower, A., *History of the University of Edinburgh, 3 vols* (1817–30)

Catalogue of the Graduates in the Faculties of Arts, Divinity and Law of the University of Edinburgh since its Foundation (1858)

Dalziel, A., *History of the University of Edinburgh*, 2 vols (1862)

Donaldson, G. (ed.), *Four Centuries: Edinburgh University Life, 1583–1983* (1983)

Footman, R., and Young, B., *Edinburgh University: An Illustrated Memoir* (1983)

Fraser, A. G., *The Building of Old College: Adam, Playfair and the University of Edinburgh* (1989)

Grant, A., *The Story of the University of Edinburgh during its First Three Hundred Years*, 2 vols (1884)

Guild, J. R., and Law, A. (eds), *Edinburgh University Library, 1580–1980: A Collection of Historical Essays* (1982)

Horn, D. B., *A Short History of the University of Edinburgh, 1556–1889* (1967)

Morgan, A. (ed.), *University of Edinburgh Charters, Statutes and Acts of the Town Council and the Senatus, 1583–1858* (1937)

Universities Commission – Scotland. Edinburgh Evidence (*Parliamentary Papers*, 1837), vol. xxxv

BEFORE 1690

Craufurd, Thomas, *History of the University of Edinburgh from 1580 to 1646* (1808)

Durkan, J., 'The royal lectureships under Mary of Lorraine',
    Scottish Historical Review, 62 (1983)

Gunn, W. M. (ed.), *Select Works of Robert Rollock* (Wodrow
    Society, 1849)

Horn, D. B., 'The origins of the University of Edinburgh',
    Edinburgh University Journal, 22 (1966)

Kirk, J., '"Melvillian" reform in the Scottish Universities', in
    A. A. MacDonald, M. Lynch and I. B. Cowan (eds), *The
    Renaissance in Scotland* (1994)

Lynch, M., 'The origins of Edinburgh's "toun college":
    a revision article', *Innes Review*, 33 (1982)

Ouston, H., 'York in Edinburgh: James VII and the patronage
    of learning in Scotland, 1679–1688', in J. Dwyer, R. Mason
    and A. Murdoch (eds), *New Perspectives on the Politics and
    Culture of Early Modern Scotland* (1982)

Rae, T. I., 'The origins of the Advocates Library', in P. Cadell
    and A. Matheson (eds), *For the Encouragement of Learning:
    Scotland's National Library, 1689–1989* (1989)

Shepherd, C., 'Newtonianism in Scottish universities in the
    seventeenth century', in R. H. Campbell and A. S. Skinner
    (eds), *The Origins and Nature of the Scottish Enlightenment*
    (1982)

1688–1832

Anderson, R. G., and Simson, A. D. C. (eds), *The Early Years of
    the Edinburgh Medical School* (1976)

Burton, J. H. (ed.), *The Autobiography of Dr Alexander Carlyle of
    Inveresk, 1722–1805* (1910)

Cairns, J., 'Rhetoric, language, and Roman law: legal educa-
    tion and improvement in eighteenth-century Scotland',
    Law and History Review, 9 (1991)

Doig, A. (ed.), *William Cullen and the Eighteenth Century
    Medical World* (1993)

Emerson, R. L., 'Scottish universities in the eighteenth
    century', *Studies in Voltaire and the Eighteenth Century* (1977)

Hannay, R. K., 'The Visitation of the College of Edinburgh, 1690', *Book of the Old Edinburgh Club*, viii (1916)

Morrell, J. B., 'Practical Chemistry in the University of Edinburgh 1799–1843', *Ambix* (1969)

Rosner, L., *Medical Education in the Age of Improvement: Edinburgh Students and Apprentices, 1760–1826* (1991)

Sher, R. B., *Church and University in the Scottish Enlightenment: The Moderate Literati of Edinburgh* (1985)

Sher, R. B., 'Professors of Virtue', in M. A. Stewart (ed.), *Studies in the Philosophy of the Scottish Enlightenment* (1990)

1832 TO THE PRESENT

Anderson, R. D., *Education and Opportunity in Victorian Scotland: Schools and Universities* (1983)

Barfoot, M., 'To ask the suffrages of the patrons': *Thomas Laycock and the Edinburgh chair of medicine, 1855* (1995)

Catto, I. (ed.), 'No spirits and precious few women': *Edinburgh University Union, 1889–1989* (1989)

Fenton, C., 'Appleton's architects: the University of Edinburgh, 1949–65' (Edinburgh University PhD, 2002)

Foulkes, G. (ed.), *Eighty Years On: A Chronicle of Student Activity in the University of Edinburgh during the Eighty Years of the Existence of the Students' Representative Council* (1964)

Hall, J. T. D., *The Tounis College: An Anthology of Edinburgh University Student Journals, 1823–1923* (1985)

Horn, D. B., 'The Universities (Scotland) Act of 1858', *University of Edinburgh Journal*, 19 (1958–60)

Macpherson, J. I., *Twenty-one Years of Corporate Life at Edinburgh University: Being a Short History of the Students' Representative Council and an Account of its Majority Celebrations* (c. 1905)

Quasi cursores: Portraits of the High Officers and Professors of the University of Edinburgh at its Tercentenary Festival (1884)

Records of the Tercentenary Festival of the University of Edinburgh celebrated in April 1884 (1885)

Stodart-Walker, A. (ed.), *Rectorial Addresses Delivered before the University of Edinburgh, 1859–1899* (1900)

Turner, A. L. (ed.), *History of the University of Edinburgh, 1883–1933* (1933)

University of Edinburgh, *Three Hundred and Fiftieth Anniversary, 1583–1933: Records of the Celebration* (1933)

Usher, C. M. (ed.), *The Story of Edinburgh University Athletic Club* (1966)

Wright, D. F., and Badcock, G. D. (eds), *Disruption to Diversity: Edinburgh Divinity, 1846–1996* (1996)

INDEX

Page numbers in *italics* refer to illustrations.